CLEAR & SIMPLE

HOW TO HAVE CONVERSATIONS THAT LEAD TO CONVERSION

BY ANDRÉ REGNIER

Nihil Obstat: Fr. Richard Jaworski, CC
               Censor Deputatus
               May 29, 2018

Imprimatur: † Most Reverend Terrence Prendergast, S.J.
               Archbishop of Ottawa

               Ottawa, Ontario | June 8th, 2018
               Solemnity of the Most Sacred Heart of Jesus

Catholic Christian Outreach
1247 Kilborn Pl
Ottawa ON K1H 6K9
cco.ca

Printed in the United States of America
ISBN-13: 978-1-928144-96-0

For St. Francis Xavier

"Pray to the Lord of the harvest that He send forth labourers into His harvest."
— **Matthew 9:38**

TABLE OF CONTENTS

Clear and Simple

I had the good fortune of meeting André Regnier nearly twenty-five years ago. He and his wife Angèle were five years into what has become their life's work of raising up a new generation of young missionary disciples on university campuses across Canada and beyond. From the start, André has been compelled by a single-hearted devotion to not only share the love of Jesus with others but to rediscover Jesus' strategy for making disciples. This means leading others to encounter Jesus, but also accompanying them and forming them into mature disciples, who can in turn make disciples.

André has written a timely and important book. It addresses what the recent popes have repeatedly underlined as the Church's top priority: the direct engagement of all the baptized in the New Evangelization. It also provides a very practical and comprehensible answer to the one question that both clergy and laity are asking: how to do the work of the New Evangelization?

In answering this question, this book lays out the essential elements of Jesus' disciple-making strategy in a step-by-step process, moving from encounter, to conversion, to accompaniment and formation, and finally to missionary multiplication. With unique insight acquired from thirty years of field-tested experience, André succeeds in one of his stated goals for the book: to "demystify" the whole process of evangelization, thereby making evangelization accessible to every person in the pew.

In his Apostolic Exhortation, *The Joy of the Gospel*, Pope Francis challenged the Church to "dream of a 'missionary option'" that would create "a missionary impulse capable of transforming" her whole life. André has answered that challenge in his own life. He and his fellow lay missionaries in Catholic Christian Outreach have found a way to live that dream, and to help hundreds of others make the dream of a missionary option a reality in their own lives.

I pray that as you read this book, the Lord Jesus will awaken in your heart a deep missionary impulse to take up your place in the Great Commission, and give you the courage to become a disciple who makes disciples.

Peter Herbeck
Vice-President and Mission Director
Renewal Ministries

INTRODUCTION: A SIMPLE CONVERSATION

Recently, I spoke at a parish where the crowd was mostly retired folks. I had come to speak to them about the ministry I co-founded, Catholic Christian Outreach (CCO), a ministry of evangelization and formation working on university campuses. While I was excited to share my insights into the ways the Lord was reaching university students through our ministry, I wasn't sure how much of this good news would resonate with my audience that day. My initial thought was, "Will these older adults be interested in hearing about the spiritual reality on university campuses?"

I talked about how we, the Church, are losing so many of our young people when they go to university. I longed for these older parishioners to understand the significance of this loss for the Church. These students were our future leaders—doctors, politicians, teachers, inventors—and, more fundamentally, each of them was a soul precious to the Lord. My heart ached for each of these "lost sheep" who wandered away from the fold without being invited to respond to the Lord's call to be his disciples. I wanted my audience to share my heart for the lost. But were the struggles of young people too far removed from their own experiences?

After my presentation, one lady came rushing up to me. She approached me with urgency, almost desperation. She began to explain how she had nine children—all very intelligent, well-mannered and raised in the Church. She described how all her boys were altar servers and two of them, as kids, had wanted to be priests. She said everything seemed right as her children left home—with faith in hand—to become lawyers and doctors. "But today, none of them go to Church anymore," she told me.

By this point, a crowd had gathered around us. The grandmothers among them nodded. They all shared her pain. They, too, had seen their children wander away. She went on to say, "I have 25 grandchildren. I don't know if there is one who is even interested in the Church." She explained how her parish priest, and even the whole community, once regarded her family as the model Catholic family. "My husband no longer believes. And to my shock, many of my brothers and sisters who I thought had faith also no longer practice, save for one brother. He's Christian, but he's no longer Catholic." After unloading her broken heart, she sighed. "What did I do wrong?"

It wasn't a rhetorical question. She looked to me for an answer, as did the rest of the small crowd.

I have an answer. It's not a matter of what we did wrong, but of what we Catholics, by and large, haven't yet learned to do.

And it's something very simple: having *intentional spiritual conversations*.

I realize that, at first, the concept of "intentional spiritual conversations" might not sound particularly simple. While all of us understand the idea of "conversation," we might be uncertain about what it would mean to have *intentional spiritual* conversations or how to go about initiating them.

To be sure, there's much to unpack in this idea. But I'll begin with this assertion: Intentional spiritual conversations are not as intimidating as you might think. Our missionaries and students have proven this to us again and again. Furthermore, as we've discovered over the last 30 years of evangelization on campus, we, as Catholic evangelists, are most effective and fruitful when we build up leaders in the context of relationships.

In CCO's ministry, we choose to make contact with students not via brochures, posters or announcements, but through good, old-fashioned one-on-one conversations. In these conversations, it has always been our clear intention to evangelize; but to evangelize intentionally, we need to do more than say, "You should love God," or, "Go to Church." It's crucial that we be equipped with or have available a simple and clear presentation of an evangelistic message. To build up our leaders, we have to go beyond words of encouragement. We need to provide them with intentional accompaniment for their spiritual growth.

Let me share with you a real-life example: Jeff, a first-year student at the University of Saskatchewan, was one of the first young men I met as a CCO missionary. Sitting down together each week, we got to know each other. Early on, he expressed how bored and uninspired he was going to Mass on Sundays. He was frustrated, but he had hope: He was going on a weekend retreat, intending to rediscover his faith.

We met in the university cafeteria two days after the retreat. I asked him, "Did you find what you were looking for?" He was disappointed; he hadn't. In fact, he was even more confused about his faith now than before the retreat.

I sensed a real desire from him to believe—to have more faith. With clear intentionality to evangelize, I said, "I believe I know what you're looking for." With his permission, I shared the *kerygma*, the basic message of the Gospel. I explained it clearly and simply, so he could understand: I told Jeff that God had made him for a loving, personal relationship with him. That relationship had been broken through sin—both Jeff's own sin and the effects of original sin. But this was not the final word of the story: God the Father, out of his unfathomable love, sent his only Son, Jesus Christ, to atone for these sins and to restore Jeff's relationship with God. Now the Lord was waiting only for Jeff's freely given "yes" to God's plan for him.

In that noisy cafeteria, where intense background activity surrounded us, I asked him a question. It's the most important question, the one I felt he was asking himself: "Would you like to put your faith, however small at this moment, in Jesus Christ by placing him at the centre of your life?"

Through God's grace, without hesitation, Jeff said, "Yes! This is what I want." We prayed together, inviting Jesus to have full access to Jeff's heart.

I immediately celebrated his decision and affirmed its spiritual significance in his life. I encouraged him to pray, read the Scriptures and go to Confession. I assured him that Mass was going to be a significantly different experience for him.

The next week, Jeff had news for me: his faith had come alive. He described how the Mass was different for him as he joined the singing and listened to the readings, the Gospel and the homily. At one point he was so moved, so filled with love and joy, that he felt like standing up and shouting, "Jesus!" I was slightly relieved that he'd shown restraint at that moment instead of interrupting the Holy Mass—but I was overjoyed that the name of Jesus was erupting within him.

To support and encourage Jeff's newfound faith, we talked regularly about how Jeff could grow in his love for God. I also saw in Jeff leadership qualities which, if intentionally developed, could help him share his faith more effectively with others. I made it my goal to help him recognize and make use of those talents in his own journey with Christ.

That was 20 years ago, and Jeff's zeal for his relationship with Jesus has not waned. Rather, Jeff Lockert, as president of CCO, has remarkable influence in Canada and throughout the world.

For decades, CCO has been equipping missionary disciples, especially our staff and students, to have intentional and life-changing conversations. Campus has always been our primary mission, but the field is so much bigger than campus. My hope is that every Catholic, in embracing their missionary identity, would be able to initiate intentional spiritual conversations with the people in their lives. Here's my favourite example: If you were sitting in a coffee shop with a good friend and they said, "I want the kind of faith that you have," and you had 10 minutes to respond, what would you say?

I've probably asked thousands of people this question over the years. And the overwhelming response? "I don't know." Most people don't feel confident navigating this conversation. They understand that evangelization is necessary, but struggle when it comes to understanding how to live it out practically. I can't count the number of times that, after giving a talk, great crowds of flustered parents, grandparents and young people flock to me, wanting to know what they could have said differently to their friend, family member, co-worker, etc. Their desire to lead others to Christ is solid, but exercising this desire is a much more daunting task.

And it's everybody: The parish priest feels lost as to how to make his homilies evangelistic. Parishioners leading sacramental preparation know most of their program participants will not come back after receiving the sacraments. Youth ministers, diocesan coordinators, and heads of ministries don't know how to implement a program that effectively evangelizes. They each have an evangelist's heart, longing to see the people in front of them fully embrace Christ. Often, though, they're faced with a disheartening scene: their many efforts seem to amount to so little.

This experience has a devastating effect: a popular understanding that there isn't a concrete, effective way to evangelize. That's wrong! Let's begin, right now, building a new understanding: Effective evangelization is possible.

Since his Ascension, the Lord's plan for his people has been that we would "make disciples of all nations" (Matthew 28:19)—that is, we who have heard the good news would go out and share it with others, equipping them to share it in turn. We are to accompany, with loving and faithful intentionality, the people in our lives as they journey towards the Lord, so that they can *personally encounter* Jesus and become *disciples of Christ.*

Many faithful Catholics, however, struggle to understand what, concretely, the Church means by "disciple of Christ" or "personal encounter with Christ," and exactly what kind of evangelical activity is expected of them, as well as how this should fit into their life of faith. I would argue that this isn't their fault. Rarely is the call to encounter and to mission framed in concrete, specific terms that the average Catholic can put into practice. My hope is that this book will help fill that gap.

I am writing this book for you, and for the person God has led you to. As you keep reading, I invite you to think of a certain person. It could be a friend, a colleague or even a member of your family. Imagine yourself in that conversational situation with them, then open yourself to how God might want to speak to them through you.

CHAPTER 1:
LET'S BE CLEAR

In 2014, Angele and I were invited to participate in the World Congress of Lay Movements and Associations. It was hosted in Rome by the Congregation of the Laity, and the theme was "Culture of Encounter." Over the course of their presentations, some of the most influential global leaders in the Church consistently put forth potentially unfamiliar terms and ideas: *Personal relationship. Personal encounter with Christ.*

It was surprising to Angele and I how comfortable the universal Church was using these terms. For years, in our ministry, we'd encountered reluctance among many Catholics to emphasize the importance of a "personal relationship" with the Lord. Now, suddenly, it seemed this was the accepted language and practice in the Church. While it was very encouraging to hear people using such terms, I was straining to hear somebody define what it *meant* to have a personal relationship with Jesus Christ, or how such a relationship might come about. Did we all understand and agree on what we were talking about?

After the last presentation, I mustered up the courage to ask a question. To give you some context, we were in a large room packed with the leaders of some of the most prominent and established lay movements within the Church. Furthermore, it seemed to me that most people who'd gone to the microphone to ask a question over the course of the Congress had instead presented their own short talk! I, meanwhile, only had a short question, one that seemed terribly basic.

I approached the microphone. With a shaking voice, I said, "There's been a lot of talk about 'personal relationship' and 'encounter,' but how do I know if I've had one? How can we know if someone hasn't had an encounter? If I desire an encounter, how do I have one?"

After I'd asked my questions, the crowd broke into enthusiastic applause. Who knows—maybe people were just relieved my question was so short. But I sensed something else, based on the number of people who gave me a thumbs up or a nod: There was an appreciation that I asked questions that needed to be answered.

Afterwards, we had many follow-up conversations with the same theme: excitement over people whose lives had been changed when they met Christ, mixed with confusion about how it all happens. One such conversation occurred at dinner with two older gentlemen. They were from one of the more established and influential international lay communities. After a few moments of me struggling to speak Italian, they graciously switched to English and quickly went to the question I asked in the last session.

They affirmed the ambiguity that surrounds the Catholic understanding of conversion, and they shared how they've worked to help bring their members to deepen their faith and to share that faith with others. Encouraged by what I heard, I asked, "How do you teach them? What do you do to clarify conversion?"

After a long explanation, which focused on good catechesis and the fundamentals of the faith (sacraments, tradition, saints, prayer, etc.), one of them stopped. He had barely mentioned initial conversion. Reluctant to give up here, I asked, "How do you bring members of your community to a place of personal encounter with Jesus Christ?" They replied with a description of how they host retreats for new people, and how, often, the participants and their families are profoundly impacted.

Their explanation of the retreat, powerful as it was, left me unclear on what it meant to have an encounter. Did the people who came to the retreat already have a personal relationship with Jesus Christ? Did they experience conversion at the retreat? How would we know? What was the message that led them to conversion? What did God do? How did people make themselves open to God?

I realize this kind of questioning might seem a bit excessive. It's not that I doubted people's experience. I was trying to be clear on what was going on with the hope that the Church could learn and implement the principles of conversion.

St. Augustine made a related point in his own writing when he said, "What then is time? If no one asks me, I know what it is. If I wish to explain it to him who asks, I do not know" (*Confessions*).

How would you respond if you were asked, "What is evangelization? Conversion? Encounter?" I suspect most Catholics would claim they understood what these words meant. But if pressed for details, most people seem to get lost in obscure ideas or expand on concepts that are not exactly evangelization—catechesis, for example.

Until there is clarity of meaning and practice and a well-defined vocabulary, the essentials of evangelization will, for the most part, be limited to new movements and communities in the Church—those that have devoted themselves in the clearest terms to the New Evangelization. For the rest of the Church, evangelization will remain primarily a subject of spiritual chatter and sentiment. It will lack potency in terms of people's real ability to share the faith.

How can ordinary Catholics begin to understand these elusive concepts more clearly? I'm confident this is a real possibility. I'd like to propose that we already have a simple yet profound icon of conversion in a familiar human experience. Accessing the idea of conversion through this living icon will help us get a concrete sense of what conversion is and how we can help others experience it.

MARRIAGE, THE ICON OF ENCOUNTER

The greatest manifestation of encounter in human terms is that between husband and wife. There is no more intimate and transformative human relationship than this lifelong, life-giving one between a man and a woman. While some individual experiences of marriage may be marred by brokenness, each of us has some sense of the Church's ideal of marriage, and each of us has some practical insight into what marriage means—both the wedding ceremony and the lifelong, lived reality of holy matrimony.

I'm reminded of this every year. Working with a youth movement in the Church, I have the blessing of attending *a lot* of weddings. There's nothing like the joy of the marriage sacrament when it's celebrated by two people in love with Christ and his Church; two people surrounded by supportive, faithful friends committed to encouraging the young couple in their vocation.

One priest came to me, almost in tears, after marrying two of our students. He admitted that, more often than he wished, he found it difficult to celebrate the marriage sacrament with the proper sense of joy and hope, as he knew that so many couples he married had no intention of coming back to Mass until they had a child to baptize. But with our students, his sorrow had turned to wonder and awe. In the case of these two young people who understood the sacrament and who were prepared to put Christ at the centre of their lives together, he was filled with hope, and with a sense of the day's sacred character. "This is the way it's supposed to be!" he exclaimed.

Such is the image of marriage I want to keep in mind throughout this chapter. We know that the marriage sacrament involves the freely given consent of both the husband and the wife, motivated not by fear or manipulation, but by a desire for an exclusive and life-giving relationship. Each spouse receives the other individually and personally. They aren't just consenting to enter into an institution they approve of in general terms, but into a relationship with a specific, beloved person.

At the same time, each spouse needs a mature understanding of marriage as a lifelong commitment requiring generosity, chastity, humility and a willingness to work together. Marriage changes the spouses' priorities. The relationship between spouses isn't just one among many relationships in their lives. Rather, it becomes the central human relationship that affects how they relate to everyone and everything else. Their whole community—particularly the Church—is called to recognize the significance and sacredness of this choice, to affirm them in it and to support them.

In a very simple, practical, yet profound sense, then, we can begin to understand conversion by seeing marriage as the *icon of encounter* between God and his Church.

Is it presumptuous to frame our understanding of conversion in terms of marriage? Not in the least. Throughout salvation history, God has helped his people understand his desire for a relationship with them using the terms of marriage. The prophet Isaiah tells God's people, "As a young man marries a young woman, so will your Builder marry you; as a bridegroom rejoices over his bride, so will your God rejoice over you" (Isaiah 62:5). In the early days of the Church, St. Paul wrote in his letter to the Ephesians, "'For this reason a man will leave his father and mother and be joined to his wife, and the two shall become one flesh.' This is a great mystery, and I am applying it to Christ and the church" (Ephesians 5:31-32). The Catechism of the Catholic Church (CCC) further affirms, "The entire Christian life bears the mark of the spousal love between Christ and the Church" (CCC, 1617).

If the whole Christian life "bears the mark of [this] spousal love," then we can proceed confidently with this comparison. In fact, what I suggest here is that we can apply our understanding of holy matrimony to grasp more concretely what the Church means by "conversion," making us better equipped to respond to the call to evangelize. In particular, I want to focus on how this analogy captures three critical aspects of our humanity, each of which ought to be engaged for us to experience conversion: our *will*, our *intellect* and our *heart*.

THE WILL: OURS TO ACTIVATE

Let's look at the dynamics of a Catholic wedding rite. Note that I don't mean to lift an individual's initial conversion to the status of a sacrament. Rather, I want to draw out the analogous core principles that make it possible to enter into such a profound, lifelong, committed and fruitful relationship.

The Catechism of the Catholic Church states the following about both spouses consenting to marriage:

> The parties to a marriage covenant are a baptized man and woman, free to contract marriage, who freely *express their consent*; "to be free" means:
>
> • not being under any constraint; and

• not impeded by any natural or ecclesial law.

> The Church holds the exchange of consent between the spouses to be the indispensable element that "makes the marriage." *If consent is lacking, there is no marriage.* (CCC, 1625-1626, emphasis added)

Consent is an essential aspect to the nature of such a committed relationship. Without it, there is no true relationship based on love. Likewise, God will not impose, coerce or even presume our love and devotion to Him. We have to give some form of consent indicating that we are open to the relationship. God has done His part—in Christ, he proposes to us a relationship with Him that is intimate and unending. Only we can respond on our own behalf.

The Catechism goes on to say this about marriage:

> The consent must be an act of the will of each of the contracting parties, free of coercion or grave external fear. No human power can substitute for this consent. If this freedom is lacking, the marriage is invalid. (CCC, 1628)

I've seen how damaging it can be when a person's faith is coerced through fear. This became particularly clear to me back in 1988, when my parents went to a live-in Catholic retreat where they were invited to intentionally open their lives up to Jesus Christ. They both acknowledged this retreat as a turning point in their spiritual lives, an encounter with God my mother always longed for in her life. Both my parents described afterwards how faith or obedience to the Church and God had until then been inspired by fear. My father recalled countless parish missions and retreats on which he'd felt terrified by the prospect of hell.

He wasn't alone. Many people of my parents' generation have told me that fear of God and his judgement kept them going to Church every Sunday. As one lady shared with me, "Confession was not an act of repentance, but an avoidance of judgement." It's no wonder so many people of my parents' generation couldn't or didn't want to pass on a faith that was wrapped up in fear.

Similarly, the Catechism's point is that a sincere "yes" cannot be forced by fear and coercion. As Divine Providence would have it, the failure of many people of my parents' generation to pass on the faith brought my whole generation to a critical point. Catholics like me had to make a personal choice regarding how we wanted live our faith. Unfortunately, most chose to walk away from the Church. The good news is that those who chose to authentically embrace the faith were motivated by one thing: love.

I remember my parish priest sharing his observation on the matter in a homily. It grieved him that fewer young people were coming to Mass these days. But he found hope in the fact that most of those who *did* come seemed to have a powerful personal story of love and encounter with the Lord and a stronger, more active faith because of it.

I have a dream—a desire—I would like to share with you. What if every baptized Catholic had such a story?

CHOOSING FOR OURSELVES

It's not unreasonable for us to desire such a revolution of faith and encounter in the Church. God desired it first:

> The invisible God, from the fullness of his love, addresses men as his friends, and moves among them, in order to invite and receive them into his own company. The adequate response to this invitation is faith. By faith, man completely submits his intellect and his will to God. With his whole being, man gives his assent to God the revealer. Sacred Scripture calls this human response to God, the author of revelation, "the obedience of faith." (CCC, 142-143)

The same idea is expressed in *Dei Verbum*: "The obedience of faith (Rom. 13:26; see 1:5; 2 Cor 10:5-6) is to be given to God … [with believers] *freely assenting* to the truth revealed by Him" (emphasis added).

The element of choice should never be overlooked. While it's true that, if we're baptized as infants, the assent of parents and godparents on our behalf is sufficient at the time, each of us is called to give our own "assent" or "submission" to God as we become capable of reason and judgement. When accompanying another person on their spiritual journey, we need to ask this question: Has this person ever given a free, mature "yes" to the offer of a relationship with God through Christ?

MAKE NO ASSUMPTIONS

Because this choice to respond to God's invitation is so important, *we must never simply assume that someone has made it*. Doing so would mean failing to serve and evangelize the Catholics who come to Mass regularly (sadly, only a small fraction of baptized Catholics in our country), but who may never have made a clear choice to become disciples of Christ. It would also mean neglecting the "lost sheep" who have wandered away from the fold. Many such people, in my experience, have left not because they've deliberately rejected the Gospel, but because no one has ever clearly presented them with the offer of a relationship with God through Christ.

Once again, we see an analogous truth expressed in the sacrament of marriage, in which the Church never simply assumes a couple have chosen each other for life just because they live together. The commitment—an unambiguous "yes"—is indispensable to allowing the two to become one.

A similar consent is involved in our entering into a relationship with Jesus: "Conversion means accepting, *by a personal decision*, the saving sovereignty of Christ and becoming his disciple" (*Redemptoris Missio*, emphasis added). There needs to be consent, informed by the intellect and desire and given freely by the will, to give our lives fully to Jesus Christ. We see in the words of Pope Benedict XVI that our initially choosing Christ is essential to our conversion:

> Conversion is not simply a moral decision that corrects the way we live, but it is a choice of faith that draws us fully into intimate communion with the living and concrete person of Jesus ... Conversion is the total "yes" of those who surrender their lives to the Gospel, responding freely to Christ. (General Audience, February 17, 2010)

"A choice of faith ... a total yes" is what God, through his Church, is inviting people to offer. It's the choice that we, as participants in the New Evangelization, are likewise inviting people to make. But how, exactly, does someone give that consent?

A HUMAN ACT: THE SIGNIFICANCE OF A SIMPLE "YES"

Here's a story that illustrates how simple this "yes" can be. I make a point to visit campuses where CCO missionaries are active in ministry. Recently, while I was at Queen's University, I joined a small group of young adults who were meeting at the Newman House, a Catholic chaplaincy building. They were going through the final lesson of the *Discovery* faith study. I asked them how they were enjoying the study. The faith study leader smiled and, with her eyes, encouraged the others to speak up. One by one, they shared how they had placed Christ at the centre of their lives during the previous week's faith study meeting. They articulated how their lives have been profoundly impacted by this decision. I could barely contain my joy!

In that moment, I was struck by extraordinary events in an ordinary setting. The room wasn't remarkable, and the members of the group were sitting quite casually around a table. They weren't in a spectacularly sacred space, or even a quiet space—laughter and conversation were very audible from the room next to us. And that room was special in its commonness, because faith study groups like this one meet in rooms like that one all across the country. Conversion and encounter are not determined by environment, but by God's grace and our will.

If we're at all skeptical about what God can do with a simple "yes," we need only recall what is perhaps the most important "yes" ever given by a person to God: Mary's *fiat*. "Here I am, the servant of the Lord," Mary said to the archangel Gabriel, after hearing the Lord's invitation to bear the Son of God; "let it be with me according to your word" (Luke 1:38). With her assent, simply and humbly expressed, the Lord was incarnate in human history. The world would never be the same.

While the Lord had chosen his Mother from before all ages and prepared her in secret for that awesome role, the Gospel account of the Annunciation doesn't suggest God chose to send his angel to her in a moment that was otherwise marked by ceremony or particularly special to human eyes. In the midst of a seemingly ordinary day, Mary was asked to make an extraordinary choice. So it is in many of our lives, and so it may be in the lives of people we're called to evangelize.

If we're still not sure why a clear, simple "yes" matters so much, let's return to the analogy of marriage. The Catechism tells us, regarding marriage, that

> ... consent consists in a "human act by which the partners mutually give themselves to each other": "I take you to be my wife"—"I take you to be my husband." This consent that binds the spouses to each other finds its fulfillment in the two "becoming one flesh." (CCC, 1627)

Saying "yes" is a human act that opens our hearts to Christ, who has already given himself to us. Using clear words, in the sacrament of holy matrimony, "I take you ..." becomes a human act of mutual consent that binds one spouse to the other. Clear expressions are fundamental to the sacrament of holy matrimony, and to all sacraments.

The same is true in so many aspects of our lives. Words are important. They express our intention, not just our emotions. Think of the case of a man's proposal to the one he loves. He isn't just looking for a smile, an expression of gratitude or sentimental words. He's seeking, first and foremost, a concrete and unquestionable "yes."

Similarly, God shows us His love in the sacraments, Scriptures, community, Eucharistic Adoration and in countless other ways. The response of one who experiences conversion is not simply appreciation, emotionality and gratitude for this love. Conversion means going beyond expressing how good we feel, how much we appreciate the Church's wisdom or how we have been so encouraged, healed, restored, etc. In conversion, we *reciprocate*, responding to the Lord's proposal with similar commitment and consent. We surrender our whole lives to Christ and begin to live in a new way.

This isn't necessarily the common understanding. Often, our evangelization efforts in the Church go only as far as sentimentality or intellectual stimulation. Perhaps the participants in a parish event tell us that they loved the spiritual experience the event provided or that they enjoyed feeling close to God. But their account gives no indication of personal response or consent. They're grateful for the experience, but they've missed the chance to respond to an invitation and commit their lives to Christ.

Alternatively, perhaps participants in catechetical formation or theology programs express satisfaction at learning more and more about the Catholic faith, but without ever indicating a sense that they see the Gospel message as a living, personal invitation requiring a concrete response from them specifically, and with the power to transform their lives. Such cases also represent a missed opportunity to call these participants to conversion.

IT'S MORE THAN A FEELING

If our parishioners and community members are not able to give a clear and personal "yes" to the invitation of the Gospel, then we must ask ourselves if conversion is really taking place. As evangelists, we need to look beyond creating positive experiences, and commit to a clear intention: to call forth true consent, instead of mere theoretical approval or sentimentality.

For example, one classic starting point in Catholic evangelical efforts is to bring people to Jesus in Eucharistic Adoration. The hope and intention are that as participants gaze upon Jesus, they will recognize him and desire a deeper relationship with him. They might receive healing, turn away from their old lifestyle or be comforted in a difficult moment. Eucharistic Adoration represents a potentially life-changing encounter with God, and one which I have personally witnessed bring healing, comfort and restoration.

But I've also seen how the encounter's depth can sometimes be limited. On some occasions, people have described their experience to me by saying, "I felt peace, joy. I felt loved. God spoke to me." These things are very good! But they fall far short of what such an encounter could and should be. Such responses are not equivalent to conversion any more than pleasant feelings of gratitude and love towards another person are equivalent to marriage.

Compare the level of commitment, maturity and intentionality between these two responses: On the one hand, someone smiling and feeling grateful; on the other, a soul who cries out, "Lord, I recognize that you love me, but I have not loved you back. I thank you for Jesus who died for me and has shown me mercy. I open my life up to you as you did for me. Here I am, Lord."

A clear "yes" changes everything.

INTELLECT: HAVING CLARITY ABOUT WHAT WE ARE SAYING "YES" TO

Let's return to the analogy with the sacrament of marriage. As the Catechism of the Catholic Church explains,

> So that the "I do" of the spouses may be a free and responsible act and so that the marriage covenant may have solid and lasting human and Christian foundations, preparation for marriage is of prime importance. [...] It is imperative to give suitable and timely instruction to young people, above all in the heart of their own families, about the dignity of married love, its role and its exercise, so that, having learned the value of chastity, they will be able at a suitable age to engage in honorable courtship and enter upon a marriage of their own. (CCC, 1632)

It is not enough that a couple desire to be together and be willing to say "yes" to each other in front of a congregation. They need some degree of understanding about what marriage actually *is*. Otherwise, their "I do" cannot be "a free and responsible act." Similarly, a person's ability to respond freely to the invitation of the Gospel is compromised if they haven't heard and understood what that invitation actually is.

Consent presumes that all parties know what they're consenting to. This point is key. Just consider what we, as evangelists, are inviting people to do. A decision for Christ is a life-changing decision. We're inviting a person to "...commit his whole self freely to God, offering the full submission of intellect and will to God... freely assenting to the truth revealed by Him ..." *(Dei Verbum)*. To make such a commitment, the person must be clear on what the "truth revealed" to them actually is, and desire to live in that truth.

It's worth reiterating this point. No one can say "yes" in an authentic way to the Gospel if they haven't heard it proclaimed. We can't consent if we don't know what we're consenting to. As St. Paul writes, "But how are they to call on one in whom they have not believed? And how are they to believe in one of whom they have never heard? And how are they to hear without someone to proclaim him?" (Romans 10:14).

Later in this book, we'll look at practical ways to effectively share the Gospel in a spiritual conversation; for now, a more general overview will suffice.

SIMPLICITY: THE ULTIMATE SOPHISTICATION

It is very common for our evangelization efforts to be obscured by a piling on of doctrine and devotion. This is something Pope Francis wrote of in *Evangelii Gaudium*: "Pastoral ministry in a missionary style is not obsessed with the disjointed transmission of a multitude of doctrines to be imposed" (35).

I fully agree with Pope Francis on this point. That is to say, I believe strongly in the eternal truth that has been given to us by the Church, and I also appreciate the various devotions that make it possible for me to grow and live out my faith. In fact, I appreciate the Church's doctrines and devotions all the more because of my relationship with God and, in a particular way, with Jesus Christ. This relationship provides me with the grace to understand and love Church teachings more deeply. Yet, as Pope Francis stressed, "The biggest problem is when the message we preach seems identified with those secondary aspects ... [which,] important as they are, do not convey the heart of Christ's message. We need to be realistic and not assume that our audience understands the full background to what we are saying" (*Evangelii Gaudium*).

Many Catholics, I believe, have never heard the Gospel message pronounced in clear and simple terms. In other words, they've never encountered the *kerygma* (a Greek word meaning "preaching," and which the Church uses to mean "the essential Gospel message"). As my story about Jeff at the start of this book shows, hearing this simple message can be life-changing. It has the power to free us to say "yes" to Christ.

It's important to define what we mean by simplicity in our proclamation of the *kerygma*. I don't mean to suggest a simplistic approach that undermines the theological depth of the Gospel. Quite the opposite, in fact. It takes a lot of hard work to present something complex in a way that can be understood and experienced simply.

St. John Paul II, in *Redemptoris Missio*, expressed this idea with brilliant clarity. It's worth considering an extended excerpt from this text:

> In the complex reality of mission, initial proclamation has a central and irreplaceable role, since it introduces man "into the mystery of the love of God, who invites him to enter into a personal relationship with himself in Christ" and opens the way to conversion. Faith is born of preaching, and *every ecclesial community draws its origin and life from the personal response of each believer to that preaching.* Just as the whole economy of salvation has its center in Christ, so too all missionary activity is directed to the proclamation of his mystery...
>
> *The subject of proclamation is Christ who was crucified, died and is risen:* through him is accomplished our full and authentic liberation from evil, sin and death; through him God bestows "new life" that is divine and eternal. This is the "Good News" which changes man and his history, and which all peoples have a right to hear. This proclamation is to be made within the context of the lives of the individuals and peoples who receive it. It is to be made with an attitude of love and esteem toward those who hear it, in language which is practical and adapted to the situation. In this proclamation the Spirit is at work and establishes a communion between the missionary and his hearers, a communion which is possible inasmuch as both enter into communion with God the Father through Christ ...
>
> *Evangelization will always contain—as the foundation, centre and at the same time the summit of its dynamism—a clear proclamation that, in Jesus Christ ... salvation is offered to all people, as a gift of God's grace and mercy.* All forms of missionary activity are directed to this proclamation ... (emphasis added)

Can we honestly say that Jesus Christ is clearly proclaimed in our parishes, or even in our personal evangelical efforts? Many Catholics cannot. Even fewer might be able to say their proclamation of Christ is accompanied by a clear and concrete invitation for the listener to respond. The task for many of us, and the goal of the latter part of this book, will be to consider ways to bring this about.

As an additional point on the topic of the intellect and true consent, we should affirm that the lifestyle changes which necessarily result from conversion can't be swept under the carpet. As a disciple of Christ, one cannot continue to live a lifestyle that contradicts the Ten Commandments or Church teaching. Withholding this truth from someone, or misleading them in this regard in an attempt to make their "yes" come more easily, is not only uncharitable and unjust, but it also compromises the legitimacy of their consent. Their "yes," in such a case, is not "free and responsible." The process of the proclamation must present truthfully what it means to live a Christ-centred life. It must also make it clear that the person has the freedom to say "no."

Of course, a truthful proclamation of this aspect of the faith never leaves a sinner in despair. Rather, it offers a message of hope, emphasizing mercy and lifelong, ongoing conversion, for "... God proves his love for us in that *while we still were sinners* Christ died for us" (Romans 5:8, emphasis added). The Lord's invitation is not conditional on our being already perfect and free from sin—quite the contrary. He waits for our consent to cooperate with grace and be sanctified.

In our Christian journeys, each of us will reaffirm our initial "yes" to Christ, again and again, more and more deeply, as we grow closer to God. But in order to begin that journey, we need at least a basic understanding of what, and who, we're saying "yes" to.

DESIRE: THE HEART OF THE MATTER

As I was beginning work on this book, I discussed my ideas with Father Sean Wenger, CC, a priest in Ottawa, a theologian and a close friend of mine. I described to him how I wanted to help ordinary Catholics understand what the Church meant by "conversion" and how to help people experience it. Based on my experience, the main reasons I believed Catholics might not have given their "yes" to the invitation of the *Gospel* were a lack of clear proclamation (they'd never encountered the *kerygma*, or core message of the Gospel) and the absence of a concrete invitation to respond to it. In other words,

I believed it was a question of helping those we meet unite their intellect and will, so they could make a clear choice to live with Christ at the centre of their lives.

Father Sean thought this was a great start. However, he did me a huge service when he challenged my thinking ever so slightly. He said, "I agree with you that the intellect and will are necessary for authentic conversion. However, I feel it's also important to point out that the Church acknowledges the role of desire—the role of the heart."

A willed, authentic "yes" to Christ, he explained, was informed by both the mind and the heart—by the intellect and desire. This is an idea Cardinal Ratzinger (later Pope Benedict XVI) emphasized in his writing:

> Believing is not an act of the understanding alone, not simply an act of the will, not just an act of feeling, but an act in which all the spiritual powers of man are at work together. Still more: man in his own self, and of himself, cannot bring about this believing at all; it has of its nature the character of a dialogue. It is only because the depth of the soul—the heart—has been touched by God's Word that the whole structure of spiritual powers is set in motion and unites in the "yes" of believing. *(Pilgrim Fellowship of Faith)*

When we proclaim the Gospel, it's with a specific intention: to create an environment where it's possible for a person to encounter Jesus Christ intimately. Quite a feat! Thankfully, the words of the popes offer encouragement and clarity in this regard. Pope Benedict XVI, for example, tells us, "Faith is first and foremost a personal, intimate encounter with Jesus." His hope is that it would "happen to each one of us" (General Audience, October 21, 2009).

In another address, he speaks of St. Paul's "turning point." For St. Paul, the transformation of his whole being was not "the fruit of a psychological process, of a maturation or intellectual and moral development." It came from "the outside ... the fruit of his encounter with Jesus Christ." He continues even more plainly, saying, "We are only Christians if we encounter Christ ... Only in this personal relationship with Christ, only in this encounter with the Risen One do we truly become Christians" (General Audience, September 3, 2008).

As Pope Benedict XVI emphasized, "Being Christian is not the result of an ethical choice or a lofty idea, but the encounter with an event, a person, which gives life a new horizon and a decisive direction" *(Deus Caritas Est)*. Since a Christian's conviction is based not just on his intellectual grasp of an idea, but on his encounter with a living person, Jesus Christ, our "yes" is the fruit of our intellect *and* our desire. We are saying "yes" to a relationship, not just to a set of doctrines.

This also resonates with our experience in CCO. Sometimes, after a student has encountered the *kerygma* through the *Discovery* faith study or in conversation with one of our missionaries, they've attained a new level of clarity about the message of the Gospel. Still, they might not feel immediately ready to give their full "yes" to Christ. At this point, they know what the Church says the Lord is offering them, but perhaps they don't yet trust God, or haven't encountered him in a loving, personal way. What we often see is that after encountering the Lord in Eucharistic Adoration, which we invite students to do as they complete their faith studies, these students finally feel prepared to give their lives fully to Christ and begin to walk as his disciples.

While it's crucial that these students understand what the invitation to conversion means (which is why we preach the *kerygma*), it's equally important that their hearts be moved to desire it. Finally, they can unite their will with their intellect and desire and make a heartfelt, informed choice to place Christ at the centre of their lives.

Let us return to the idea of marriage as the icon of conversion. An essential quality of the marriage relationship is a desire for greater intimacy with an individual person. The encounter with the beloved moves a person to "leave his father and mother and be joined to his wife," to alter the entire arrangement of his life, so that he can say, like the lover in the Song of Songs, "I am my beloved's and my beloved is mine."

Similarly, Christian discipleship involves the heart, the desire. For instance, there are those in the Church who have given their intellectual assent to the faith. They believe that what the Church teaches is true. It is very good for anyone to have come to this place of intellectual assent. Still, there are many who testify, following a deeper encounter with Christ and a heartfelt "yes" to the personal invitation of the Gospel, that, previously, their faith had lacked a personal, incarnate dimension. Their faith became alive and ever-deepening following this personal encounter which freed them to give an authentic "yes" not only to abstract ideas, but to a relationship with the living person of Jesus Christ.

CLARITY ABOUT THE TIMING OF CONVERSION: INITIAL AND ONGOING CONVERSION

Is there a danger in placing too much emphasis on this initial "yes" to the Lord's invitation? Some readers may wonder if this truly reflects an orthodox Catholic understanding of conversion. After all, growth in holiness is a lifelong journey. The idea deserves further clarification.

The Catholic Church defines conversion not merely as a one-time event that happens when we give our first "yes" to Christ's plan. As we strive to live our lives in relationship with Christ and his Church, we should be experiencing *ongoing conversion* of our hearts and lives. That is to say, as we are drawn into deeper intimacy with the Lord, a more profound understanding of the Gospel, and a more sincere repentance from sin, we will turn continuously towards the Lord, allowing him to heal us and make us more and more like Christ.

At the same time, while acknowledging the importance of ongoing conversion, it is essential that there be equal acknowledgment and understanding of the need for *initial conversion*, such as is dramatically illustrated in the life stories of (for example) St. Paul or St. Augustine. Such conversion gives life and motivation to ongoing conversion. The question may be rightly asked: Could such a conversion happen instantly in the kind of evangelical encounters described later in this book? Could it happen, for instance, in a coffee shop? Isn't conversion something that takes time?

In response to this, I'll put forth three general models of how people experience initial conversion, all of which I've witnessed in my own ministry. The first is the experience of a person who, through the grace of baptism and support of family, grows up with a heart that is converted. For such a person, an authentic (if immature) "yes" to God has always been offered. The renewal and deepening of this "yes," with greater and greater maturity, understanding and love, is the journey of a lifetime. Next there are those who, perhaps through a significant life event, come (over a period of time) to a place of turning their lives back to God. They may have trouble pinpointing the exact moment they made the choice to follow Christ, but they are certain that a given period of time was the period of their conversion: their lives were plainly different before and after that time. Finally, there are those who experience what might be described as a clear and definite moment of conversion, of recognizing and responding to their need for Christ. Such conversions can be dramatic, but they are likely more common than many of us suppose.

Despite apparent disparities, these experiences are more similar than they are different. Each unites the intellect and the desire, and each reflects a free and sincere "yes" to the Lord's invitation. Regardless of the circumstances, authentic conversion will be seen in a life lived differently.

In accompanying others in their faith journeys, one challenge we face is that some Catholics who *have* experienced initial conversion—perhaps especially those whose conversion happened according to one of the first two models I described above—might never have recognized or claimed their conversion as such. Such individuals may be anxious about whether they've ever given a clear "yes" to the Lord. Instead of freely cooperating with grace in their ongoing conversion, these people might get "stuck" in their scruples, struggling to cast off lingering doubts that God has heard and received their assent to His plan; in other words, they doubt their initial "yes" was sufficient and effective. Such doubts may arise from a sense of imperfection: If I still sin, or if my faith is imperfect, can I really say I've experienced conversion?

The comparison of conversion with marriage can help alleviate the doubts of many such Catholics. Consider that a couple who have been married for fifty years almost certainly know a deeper intimacy and have a better understanding of one another than a young couple who were married last week. The newly-married couple face a lifetime of renewing and deepening their commitment to one another as they come to understand each other (and themselves) more deeply, and as circumstances challenge their commitment in unexpected ways.

All that being said, the couple who have been married a week are *no less married* than the other couple. Their "yes" in the sacrament of holy matrimony, witnessed by the Church, is effective. They can recall with love and gratitude the day of their wedding, understanding it as the beginning of their new life together. Regardless of any sense of imperfect intimacy, regardless of the challenges the years will bring, they have said "yes" to one another—they are married. They don't have to worry about the legitimacy of their vocation. They are free to go about the business of living it out ever more deeply, with the help of the Lord.

Similarly, Catholics who know their "yes" has been heard by God—who understand that He is faithful, even though we are imperfect—experience greater freedom in their discipleship. The call to repentance and to ever-deepening holiness and availability for God's plan never ends in this life. Still, the Catholic who can claim his initial conversion sees himself at the heart of a dynamic divine love story, and can, in a clear way, look back on his initial "yes" with awe and gratitude for God's goodness and mercy. The gift of remembering our first "yes" infuses our Christian life with vitality and purpose, and frees us to experience ongoing conversion.

Moreover, it isn't just our own faith that can be strengthened when we remember our initial conversion. If we're able to clearly communicate that story—to recount it with the intention of helping someone else reach the same point of conversion—our personal spiritual testimony can be a powerful aid to evangelization.

The idea of engaging someone in this kind of intentional spiritual conversation is something I'll cover at length later in this book. But for now, let's consider what a spiritual testimony might entail.

Typically, the structure of a testimony begins with what life was like before conversion, with particular focus on what was lacking in those days. It then leads to a description of a personal encounter with Jesus Christ and recounts how the person responded to that encounter. The ending shows how life has changed since the person gave their first "yes" to Christ.

It's incredible how moving another person's testimony can be. We see ourselves in someone else's story. We long for what they have. Our hearts can be deeply moved.

ENCOUNTER LEADING TO CONVERSION

In discussions of the New Evangelization, it's now quite accepted among Catholics that we can speak of the importance of *a personal encounter* with Jesus Christ. This gives me great joy. It is this *encounter*—a revelation of God—that opens up the way to conversion (and which is usually so central to a Christian's personal spiritual testimonies). I say it *opens up the way* to conversion because the revelation itself is not the conversion; rather, it is a point of encounter. This is a point I mean to clarify and which may help many Catholic evangelists gain a clearer understanding of conversion.

As we read in *Dei Verbum*,

> In His goodness and wisdom God chose to reveal Himself and to make known to us the hidden purpose of His will by which through Christ, the Word made flesh, man might in the Holy Spirit have access to the Father and come to share in the divine nature ... Through this revelation, therefore, the invisible God ... out of the abundance of His love speaks to men as friends ... and lives among them ... so that He may invite and take them into fellowship with Himself ...

God is constantly and actively revealing Himself, calling us into a personal friendship with the Trinity, appealing personally to our hearts and our intellects and inviting our response. We know by the testimonies of countless people that God comes to us in both life's struggles and blessings. We may hear His voice or sense His presence in nature. He might come to us as we read a good spiritual book or hear an inspiring homily. God's revelation may come in powerful, seemingly miraculous ways, or in very quiet and subtle ways. The possibilities are endless!

In each of these moments, we are invited to cooperate with the Lord, to *choose* to allow God's revelation to impact our lives so we can live our lives for Him. In other words, to give our "yes." Even powerful revelations of God's goodness and glory do not *force* us to surrender our lives to him. Rather, they open us up to the possibility of a life lived for God. The "yes" is still ours to give.

To illustrate concrete examples of initial conversion as I've described it, to distinguish between *encounter* and *conversion*, and also to help us experience the power of a personal spiritual testimony, the next section of the book introduces two specific stories of encounter with the Lord leading to conversion: First, the well-known story of St. Augustine's conversion, recounted in his spiritual autobiography, the *Confessions*. The second is a much less famous story but one without which this book would not exist. It is the story of my own initial conversion.

As you read them, I invite you to reflect on your own spiritual testimony, as well as those whose spiritual journeys you've shared.

ST. AUGUSTINE'S STORY

In St. Augustine's *Confessions*, it is striking how revelations—or encounter—become a pathway for conversion. Three areas in St. Augustine's life kept him from the knowledge and praise of God. The first was his intellectual struggle with the truths of the Christian faith, predominantly brought on by his adherence to the teachings of Manicheism. Once this barrier was overcome, the second barrier was his pride. Humbling himself to praise someone other than himself, even if that someone else was God, was a major stumbling block. Finally, even when he'd gained a heartfelt desire for the Lord, as well as an intellectual conviction that what Christians preached was true, the world and its lures and lusts of the flesh were still overwhelmingly appealing to him. He described them as chains that held him in bondage, rendering him unable to give himself to God. His will needed to be freed so he could at last give his assent to God's plan.

Most of us can relate to his struggle in some way. We see, in St. Augustine's life, how the grace of God's revelation constantly knocked at the door of his heart and mind … yet he resisted opening the door. He acknowledges in his writing that as a child he had "deeply drunk in and deeply treasured" the name of Christ, but confesses it did not take hold of him. The piety and prayers of his mother were constant reminders of the need for God.

St. Augustine grew up in a Catholic home that introduced him to Jesus. In his early years, this saint didn't understand the faith that was passed on to him. He didn't identify with it. His early introduction to Christianity did not constitute his conversion. Even when he encountered the faith in a more personal and powerful way, he recognized (as his testimony reveals) that these encounters were not, in themselves, his conversion. They were, however, God's active love leading Augustine to Himself.

It wasn't that Augustine didn't know about God before his conversion—he did. It wasn't that he didn't desire God—he did. This contradiction—between his heart's longing for love and the life that he was living—vexed him. This is important to understand, and as true today as it was fifteen hundred years ago. Remember: Just because someone comes back to Church or has a profound encounter with God does not necessarily mean they have had a life-transforming conversion—a *metanoia*.

As we know, this series of encounters, each of which opened Augustine further to the Lord, eventually did lead to his conversion. First, when Augustine read the *Hortensis*, written by the philosopher Cicero, it dramatically changed his way of thinking. This was when he desired to search for things that are beautiful and good, rather than merely the base things of the world. It was also when he began directing prayer to God.

God, in his mercy, continued to reveal himself to St. Augustine through the preaching of a bishop, St. Ambrose. In particular, Augustine heard St. Ambrose's defence of the Church's teachings—teachings which he initially despised. Through this encounter with St. Ambrose, St. Augustine had the grace to accept the validity and influence of the Scriptures and the teachings of the Church, declaring, "These things [were] safe and immovably settled in my mind." And yet, even with that certainty, St. Augustine remained unconverted.

St Augustine's struggle had long been a need to be convinced of the truth of faith. Now, his struggle was in becoming "more steadfast" in God. The ways of Christ had captured his attention and admiration, but he did not feel he had the courage to "go through its narrowness." In this place of self-awareness, he went to Simplicianus, whom he knew to be a man of faith. Simplicianus helped Augustine understand the need for humility in submitting to Christ by sharing the story of Victorinus, a well-known orator.

Victorinus, believing the truth of Christ, was asked to make a confession of faith within the Church. When Augustine heard that Victorinus "became bold against vanity and humbled before truth," Augustine's pride was exposed. Victorinus didn't want to be ashamed of Christ and chose to make his profession of faith before all the people of God.

This testimony inflamed Augustine with the longing to respond with Victorinus' courage and humility. The battle within was now a matter of *choosing* to "go through the narrowness" to be "more steadfast." He developed a new longing for such a life and he realized it was no longer "chains of lust" that held him, but rather his own "iron will." He no longer had any excuses, but he still found it impossible to surrender.

His friend Ponticianus finally helped him choose to trust completely in God's mercy. Ponticianus shared the stories of two men who converted immediately after reading the life of St. Anthony. Ponticianus pointed out that St Anthony's words instantly touched their hearts and they chose to turn away from those things of the world that had a hold on them. In a moment, they turned their lives over to the service of God.

God used this testimony to turn Augustine's thoughts inward. In those two men, Augustine saw what he was unwilling to do—give himself fully to God. Augustine cried out to a friend who was listening to this story with him, "What is the matter with us?" He saw those converts taking "heaven by force" while he continued to resist giving in to God. He recalled also how St. Anthony of the Desert heard the words of the Gospel that said, "If you wish to be perfect, go, sell your possessions, and give the money to the poor, and you will have treasure in heaven; then come, follow me"(Matthew 19:21), felt as if they were being spoken directly to him and was instantly converted.

At first, the agony of the battle within him made him retreat to the garden to weep. But then, prompted by the Holy Spirit, St. Augustine returned, opened the Scriptures and began to read the first page he landed on—a passage in St. Paul's letter to the Romans:

> Not in carousing and drunkenness, not in sexual excess and lust, not in quarreling and jealousy. Rather, put on the Lord Jesus Christ, and make no provision for the desires of the flesh. (Romans 13:13-14)

He describes the experience and the movement that happened within him: "Instantly at the end of the sentence, by a light, as it were, of serenity infused into my heart—all the gloom of doubt vanished away." In this moment, St. Augustine was free to give his heartfelt assent to the Lord, to submit to becoming a disciple of Christ. His life would never be the same.

The dramatic conversion of St. Augustine has been celebrated by many, scrutinized by others and misunderstood by most. It's universally accepted that his story of faith is extraordinary. Yes, it's extraordinary! But for many intentional disciples of Christ, we can see ourselves in St. Augustine's story of conversion, a story of turning away from an old way of living to a new life. His story is an example of someone moving from a certain point in their faith journey to a much further point, closer to the Lord, aided by the witness of others and by various encounters with God.

In the end, following his conversion, St. Augustine began to live a whole new life. St. Paul's description in his second letter to the Corinthians seems to reflect St. Augustine's experience perfectly: "[I]f anyone is in Christ, there is a new creation. Everything old has passed away; see, everything becomes new" (2 Corinthians 5:17).

ANDRÉ'S STORY

While every soul's story is unique, and while St. Augustine lived many centuries ago, aspects of his story are timeless. I recognize this clearly as I reflect on my own initial conversion.

As a young boy growing up in a Catholic family and attending Catholic schools, faith surrounded me. In my family, everything we did and celebrated seemed to revolve around the Church's liturgical calendar, focusing on feast days and religious holidays like Christmas and Easter. It was an integral part of our culture.

But even then, faith was more than culture. It involved encounter and revelation that touched me deeply. This started in the first grade. I still remember my teacher, a Sister of the Presentation of Mary, writing on the blackboard. She listed common sins, sins we could all relate to. We probably felt God's wrath because of such sins.

Then she drew the cross. With a dash of the eraser, she wiped away the list of sins and explained in simple terms that this is what Jesus did for us on the cross. I was amazed! I understood profoundly how Jesus' death and resurrection impacted my life. But a more significant encounter with God was yet to come.

It was Good Friday and I was nine years old. My parents and siblings were away visiting relatives, and I found myself at home alone. This was very rare in a family of eight kids. I curled up in a chair, picked up our family picture Bible and started going through it. I started with Genesis, moved to Abraham, Moses, David … and I just kept going.

I made my way to the New Testament, where I read about Jesus' birth, John the Baptist, the disciples on the sea, Jesus healing the blind man, the last supper and the scandal of the lashings of Christ. Then, my eyes fell on Christ hanging on the cross. I began to cry. My crying led to uncontrollable sobbing. It felt like it wasn't coming from my head or even my heart, but from my soul. It was different from any emotion I had ever experienced. I can remember feeling good about the tears. With this encounter, together with the message the sisters taught me of Jesus dying for my sins, a profound appreciation for the cross was infused into my very being.

As you read this, maybe you're picturing a pious, holy young Catholic boy. That would be false. I was not a good Catholic boy. Sure, on the inside, hidden away in my private life, I had a soft spot for Jesus. But it did not translate into my actions and my attitude towards life. My private spiritual encounters didn't seem relevant to my day-to-day life. To be honest, I thought that if I got close to God, He would ruin my life.

This hidden spirituality is a common reality for baptized Christians. The sacraments' grace enables us to be aware of God's presence and perhaps desire it in our lives. It allows us to be naturally spiritual. The problem for many—and for me at that time—is that innate spirituality does not necessarily translate into a spiritually fruitful life. This made it very easy for me to follow along with most of my peers and keep away from the Church. After graduating from high school, I "partied" for the next two years. I was having a good time and had no desire to search for meaning and purpose. But God, who is always in search of us, began to knock on the door of my life.

I was happily dating a young woman when she shocked me by saying, "It's over. I found someone else." I didn't want to give up too easily, so I fought for my place in the relationship. I asked, "What is it about him that would make you choose him over me?" (Note: Don't ever ask that question if you're not ready to hear the truth.)

She began to explain how the other guy treated her so well. It was tough to hear myself compared to him. Then she added, "He's a Christian." My quick and confident response was, "I'm a Christian, too." At that point she looked at me with a sarcastic smile and spoke the most painful words: "He's a *real* Christian."

I sat there, paralyzed by the truth. I didn't respond because I knew I had no defence. The state of my soul was revealed, and I felt the weight of it. I realized then that this was God in search of me. That moment was not one of devastation, but of stirring up desire and openness.

A month later, I decided to pack my bags and join my brother in Fort McMurray for six months of work. To be clear, my sudden departure was not motivated by the broken relationship. It was about the money. There was lots of money to be made in Alberta, and I wanted some of it.

Shortly before I left, I was spending a Sunday with friends. We were right next to the cathedral, the same one where I received all my sacraments. We were discussing what we were going to do that night and we decided to go out for dinner and then go to a movie. And here came God's second knock at my heart: My best friend told us he was going to Mass first and he would meet us for dinner after.

What a punch to the gut—it took my breath away. I was in awe of my friend: impressed, moved and envious all at the same time. Everything in me wanted to have chosen God as my first priority. At the same time, I was heartbroken and ashamed that God *wasn't* a priority in my life. Sure, I might have seen myself as inwardly spiritual. But the truth, in terms of how I lived my life, was different.

These experiences—a girl breaking up with me to date a Christian instead and my friend choosing to go to Mass before going out with the guys—were how God spoke to me. Initially, all I felt was guilt. I felt so far from God, and that was a sad and disappointing realization. Yet I also felt a sense of hope and direction. I thought maybe now that I knew what I was looking for—this relationship with God—something could change. This was an essential part of my conversion process.

But it was still very much a process; I had not yet had my conversion. This distinction shouldn't be overlooked or understated. I was in the same spot as St Augustine: My head may have been converted, but my heart and will had not been sufficiently moved. My life had yet to really change.

But God did not leave me in that place for long. The first thing I did on the Friday I arrived in Fort McMurray was look up the nearest Catholic church in the phone book. (Remember, this was a long time ago. Phone books still existed.) I called to find out the Mass times, then early on Sunday morning, I went to Mass—by myself, voluntarily. I didn't go because of guilt or somebody had told me to. I went because I *desired* it in my life. It was *my choice*, and I recognized that.

I felt so pleased with my decision to make God my first priority. I don't remember what the church looked like or what the homily was. (I am sure it was good.) What I recalled was the overwhelming sense of God's presence during the Mass. I was literally shaking as I stood in that church. I wasn't scared; I was overflowing with joy.

I see my experience at Mass that Sunday morning reflected in the words of St. Augustine, when, after reading Romans 13:13-14, he says, "No further would I read, nor did I need; for instantly, as the sentence ended—by a light, as it were, of serenity infused into my heart—all the gloom of doubt vanished away" *(Confessions)*. At that moment in church during Mass, I, too, was filled with a sense of joy and unexplainable intimacy with God. I instantly fell in love with Him.

I remember getting into my car after Mass—I began to sing! I had never done that before except when I was in church. And the songs I sang were songs I knew growing up—hymns and Christmas carols. I couldn't help myself. I wanted to sing, to worship!

My life was never the same after that. I put God first in my life: I gave him my sincere, heartfelt "yes." I began to pray and read the Scriptures more fervently. I got involved in the parish and I never missed Sunday Mass. I changed how I lived—the language I used and my purpose in life. I saw the change not as God taking anything away from me, but as God pouring down meaning and purpose, courage, discipline, joy and zeal for life.

BARRIERS TO GIVING OUR 'YES'

Consider what God can do with a person's "yes" to his plan. Our Mother Mary's *fiat* to God's plan is the supreme example of this. St. Augustine, a Doctor of the Church, has drawn souls to Christ for more than a thousand years through his testimony and teaching. Even in my own life, I've seen the incredible ways God used my "yes": When I first gave my life to God during Mass in northern Alberta, I could not have imagined founding CCO, nor could I have fathomed the ways such a movement could transform thousands of lives.

When we look at the Church today, and at her people, we recognize that not all baptized Catholics—nor even all regular Mass attendees—are currently bearing the fruits of conversion. As I've suggested throughout these previous sections, what we ultimately hope is that these people would activate their will; we hope that they will give their informed, wholehearted assent to Christ's plan for their lives.

There are, I would argue, four things that might hold them back from giving and claiming a clear "yes" to the Lord:

1. Their intellect has not been developed with respect to the Gospel—in other words, they don't know what they're saying "yes" to. Faith is primarily an emotional or sentimental experience for them. If they give a "yes" to God, it is a naive "yes."

I suspect that this category captures a great many people in our parishes. Perhaps they experience feelings of love and support in the Catholic Church, and perhaps they've heard God loves them and believe it. These are very good things! On the other hand, the people in this category cannot articulate the basic Gospel message, nor do they really understand Christ's role in their salvation. They could not share the *kerygma* clearly with a friend, nor do they recognize their need for Jesus as Saviour beyond desiring feelings of happiness and belonging.

A CCO alumna shared this story with me: A parishioner at her church, who was actively involved in liturgical ministries, was reading the story of Christ's disciples encountering him after his Resurrection on the road to Emmaus (Luke 24:13-35). Having finished the reading, this parishioner then asked my friend, "So, do some Christians believe that Jesus *literally* came back from the dead?"

My friend was understandably shocked. This woman was a practicing Catholic who professed Christ's Resurrection in the Apostles' Creed every Sunday! Despite this, she'd somehow failed to recognize that the Catholic Church truly professes Christ's Resurrection, not to mention the fact that without this profession, our faith would make little sense. "If Christ has not been raised, your faith is futile and you are still in your sins" (1 Corinthians 15:17).

Though this example might sound extreme, I suspect this experience is all too representative of many of our parishioners' faith lives. We may never recognize the extent of this problem if we don't engage in intentional spiritual conversations with one another, as I'll explain in later sections of this book.

2. They lack a heart for the Lord. They might assent to Church doctrine, but it is a kind of iron-willed "yes" that is not motivated by heartfelt desire. Their "yes" lacks love or any kind of personal dimension. It is not the kind of assent Christ is asking for.

An intellectual grasp of Church teaching is without doubt a great gift. Nonetheless, our faith is not simply a set of philosophical propositions or a wide range of theological doctrines to be grasped by the intellect. It is, above all, predicated on a response to the personal, saving love that Christ offers each one of us.

Pope Benedict XVI describes Christianity as an active encounter with a person, an event that ignites a relationship: "Christianity is not 'a new philosophy or a new form of morality,' but an encounter with the person of Christ, an event that ignites a personal relationship with him" (General Audience, September 3, 2008). A conversion not founded on a loving encounter with the Lord, or which lacks this personal, incarnate dimension of encounter, might not be an authentic conversion. Sadly, as St. John Paul II observed, "Sometimes even Catholics have lost or never had the chance to experience Christ personally: not Christ as a mere 'paradigm' or 'value', but as the living Lord, 'the way, and the truth, and the life' (John 4:16)" (cited in Personal Relationship to Jesus).

The person who finds himself in this position may be a regular Mass attendee, someone who is very familiar with Church teaching, someone who is striving with the strength of their will to come to God through the sacraments offered by the Church, but who (perhaps because of inward woundedness, or perhaps because they have never seriously considered the idea) cannot recognize in God a loving and merciful Father, nor in Christ a personal and humble Saviour. On the other hand, this might be the competent student of Christian doctrine who hasn't contended with his own profound need to be seen and loved by God, or the overworked parish catechist who has never reflected on the fact that Christ's love is transformative and personal and offered to *her*.

When such Catholics strive to live holy lives (which is, of course, very good), they may live very blamelessly, but they may also experience fatigue, numbness or discouragement, since their efforts may not be open to concrete support and refreshment from the Holy Spirit, or may not be placed in light of any personal salvific narrative. They may find themselves asking, "What's the point?" or falling into patterns of resentment or judgement of others.

Alternatively, it's possible they may not see the need to reform their lives, at least in private. Despite theoretical familiarity with Church teaching, their hearts have not been touched by the message of the Gospel, and they may not feel compelled to change their habits and live in the light of truth. Regardless, their faith is not centred on a personal, loving relationship with Christ, so their ability to grow in holiness and their availability for mission could be severely limited.

Again, we may never know that a brother or sister in the Church is living this limited experience of the faith if we don't engage in intentional spiritual conversations with them. I'll deal with this necessity in the second section of this book.

3. They have an intellectual grasp of the Gospel, and they have a heartfelt desire for the Lord, but no one has called out a response from them, so they have not given it. They see what God offers through the Church and they desire it, but they don't know how to respond or receive it. Their will has not been activated in accordance with their mind and heart.

This likely captures more of our Catholic brothers' and sisters' experiences than we imagine. It is one thing to know someone has heard the Gospel message and desires intimacy with God; it's quite another to be confident that person has responded to this desire by placing Christ at the centre of his or her life.

An experience I shared in a previous book, *Catholic Missionary Identity*, captures this reality as I've witnessed it in parishes:

> I once heard a moving homily based on the Gospel passage in which Jesus asks his disciples, "But who do you say that I am?" (Mark 8:29). The priest spoke passionately of how Jesus wants us to know him. It was clear that the purpose of this homily was to invite people into a relationship with Christ. Our hearts stirred as the priest boldly stated that we could begin this relationship today. Everyone was on the edge of their seats, ready to respond to the invitation.
>
> To our great disappointment, however, the homily ended there. The priest unintentionally over-promised and under-delivered. He wanted us to respond, but he failed to tell us how. Somehow he assumed we would already know how to respond—the reality is that we do not. When I later spoke to the priest about this homily, he said he was unaware that we were hanging on his invitation. The next week at the end of his homily, he invited each of us to kneel and pray with him a simple prayer, opening our hearts to Jesus as our Lord and Saviour.

Thankfully, in this instance, the people in this parish were invited to respond to the desire of their hearts. But how many of our brothers and sisters may have found themselves in similar situations with no one to call out a "yes" from them? This is one of the most significant opportunities presented to us in intentional spiritual conversations, as I'll discuss in the next section of this book.

4. They've never acknowledged the reality or significance of their "yes," despite having legitimately offered it. They have the intellectual knowledge of the Gospel, they have a

heart for the Lord and they've offered their consent to his plan, but they have not recognized or claimed their conversion, so they struggle to experience the freedom of sonship in the Lord.

As I explained earlier in this book, it is possible for a Christian to have experienced initial conversion without recognizing it as such. Sometimes this happens because no one witnessed their conversion or affirmed them in it. It may also happen if someone does not understand the distinction between conversion and perfection.

A CCO alumna describes her own experience in this regard:

> I was blessed as a young person to have a significant experience of being able to choose Christ while preparing for Confirmation. I already had a deep affection for Jesus, and was moved by what I understood he'd done for me on the cross. At one point in our sacramental preparation class, however, I experienced a moment of fresh clarity: I realized that what the Church taught might be true or it might not be, and that what I was being asked in Confirmation was whether I really believed what I'd been told.
>
> At that moment, in my heart, I realized that I *did* believe what the Church taught about Christ, and—silently, in that moment—I told Jesus that I believed he died for me, and that I desired to live according to God's will.
>
> This quiet, grace-filled moment infused my experience of Confirmation with significance. Not only that, I also experienced a deepening love for the Lord throughout my teen years. I could see that God was faithful and never left me. My understanding of the Gospel deepened and matured, and I was always delighted by what I learned and felt free to accept it.
>
> At the same time, though, I knew I was still a sinner. Though each new experience of God's love infused me with desire to leave all bad habits and venial sin behind and to live a life of perfect holiness, again and again I watched myself fall into familiar patterns of selfishness, laziness or pride. Compared to the saints, my faith seemed very lukewarm, and my life far from exemplary.
>
> Fast forward to university. I was taking part in a faith study led by a CCO missionary who'd spent a lot of time with me and who had a good understanding of my relationship with God. She was asking me, using one of CCO's communication tools called the "relationship diagrams," whether I would say Christ was at the centre of my life. Ruefully, I told her that I *wished* I could say yes, but that I knew

it wasn't true. When she pressed me to explain, I told her how I was still far from being the person Christ was calling me to be—I wasn't a saint yet. I thought that was what she meant by *having Christ at the centre*. If that was true, I couldn't possibly claim it reflected my life.

This missionary then gently challenged my interpretation of her question. She used the analogy of marriage. A married couple do not become un-married, she pointed out, just because one spouse fails to love the other perfectly. I understood the comparison, and suddenly I also understood what she was asking. It wasn't about whether I was perfect or not, but whether I knew my need for Christ and was prepared to live my life for him, letting him sanctify me with his love.

To this question, I could give a confident "yes." I felt a new sense of gratitude and awe for what God had done in my life: Though my own faith was far from perfect, God had always been perfectly faithful, immature though my initial assent to him might have been. I knew that Christ was my Saviour and Lord. He was walking with me and helping me become more like him, day by day. Recognizing this also helped me feel free to commit more actively to sharing the Gospel with others and to live out my missionary call: I was called to share the story of God's perfect mercy, which had never once failed me.

This student's story shows how significant it can be for someone to claim their "yes." I have no doubt there are thousands of Catholics in our parishes who experience similar uncertainties, and whose confusion about the definition of conversion prevents them from claiming their own stories and glorifying God for his role in their lives.

Intentional spiritual conversations, like the one that occurred between this student and the CCO missionary leading her faith study, present us with a unique opportunity to affirm and celebrate someone's "yes" to the Lord. They could also represent a significant step in helping Catholics receive their baptismal call to mission.

My repeated claim about the crucial significance of "intentional spiritual conversations" is about due for elaboration. Both my understanding of Catholic anthropology and my own experience as a missionary have convinced me of the truth of this claim. The rest of this book will describe in detail what I mean by this, as well as equipping readers to engage in such conversations with people in their own lives.

CHAPTER 2: CONVERSATION AND CONVERSION

In 2009, my wife Angele and I were leading a CCO summer mission in Saskatoon that focused on building missionary disciples in a parish context. I had the privilege of working with a long-time faithful parishioner—let's call her Anne—who had been involved in almost every available ministry at one time or another. Anne was aware that the parish was stagnating and felt the effects personally—her own children were no longer coming to Mass. She was convinced there needed to be a more concerted effort to reach out and bring people back to the Church. Through our conversation, it was apparent that her idea of outreach equaled bringing people back to the parish by making them feel welcome through a pleasant community.

Anne's approach wasn't wrong; it was just incomplete. My goal as I spoke with her was to help Anne see that outreach goes far beyond a warm welcome. The primary goal of outreach, I suggested, is to bring people to a personal and life-changing encounter with Jesus Christ and the Church. Can making new people feel welcome be the doorway that opens them up to conversion? Yes! But engagement in the community, I put to her, is necessarily a follow-up to evangelization.

It was at this moment that Anne became overwhelmed. As we talked about evangelization, her faith shifted profoundly. Suddenly, she started to describe her faith as pieces of a puzzle. She knew about baptism, God's love, prayer, community, Jesus dying on the cross, etc. But it wasn't until I asked her to share her faith with others that she saw how the pieces of the puzzle make up a beautiful picture. For the first time in her life, she saw the significance of Jesus' death and resurrection and how it gives meaning to all the pieces of our faith. She willingly opened up her heart and her life to Jesus Christ in a new and personal way. She became an intentional disciple that day.

This personal experience, combined with her new, clear understanding of the *kerygma*, motivated her to action. She started to talk to other people about the core of our faith, hoping to lead them to conversion and integrate them into the community. What I witnessed that day was an active Catholic leader moving from a simple, earnest desire to maintain the parish ministries and community experience to a new identity as a missionary disciple. She was now ready to invite people to encounter Jesus, he who gives life and meaning to everything else that we believe and live out as Catholics.

For me, Anne's transformation was already a highlight of that summer mission. But there was even more to the story. At the end of the summer, everyone who had been involved in the mission gathered one evening to say goodbye. Anne, with great pride, introduced me to her friend who had attended the faith study that Anne led. Anne told me she had taken up my challenge to lead a faith study with friends and parishioners.

Only one couple had accepted her invitation to the study, and she was initially disappointed. But, as Anne told me, this couple faithfully came for six weeks, even as she stumbled at times through the lessons. The study became the highlight of her week as she saw the couple become excited to learn of God's love and Jesus in a way they had never done before.

Anne's friend began to tell me how she and her husband had placed Jesus at the centre of their lives. The tears began to flow, and as they embraced each other, the moment marked a milestone: a human encounter that led to conversion, and a community being formed.

However extraordinary this experience may seem, I assure you there are many similar stories that I could share with you. We should expect, as we become more missionary, such radical spiritual transformation of our people and our communities. As St. John Paul II explains, "[M]issionary activity renews the Church, revitalizes faith and Christian identity, and offers fresh enthusiasm and new incentive. Faith is strengthened when it is given to others!" *(Redemptoris Missio)*.

The challenge before us is to understand, respect and engage in this "missionary activity" in such a way that it will bear much fruit.

MANY DO NOT KNOW

In her book *Forming Intentional Disciples*, Sherry Weddell explains how research shows that a majority of Catholics do not believe God can be known personally. She suggests that many heads of various ministries in the Church are not intentional disciples.

As I reflected on this statement, I could acknowledge it was true, based on my experience in Catholic ministry. But I also knew that the people it described hadn't gone that route on purpose. Our ministry leaders haven't chosen *not* to be intentional disciples—rather, they've never been offered the choice at all.

Weddell offers a striking anecdote that supports this idea. She asked a vocational director how many of the young men he dealt with—those who were discerning a possible call to priesthood—were already disciples. The director's response was, "None. They don't know how. No one has ever talked to them about it." That's an eye-opening reality.

The people committed to evangelization want the faith and the Church to be a life-giving experience for everybody. How do we make that possible in the most common evangelization settings? Think of retreats, adoration nights, homilies, conference small groups. What about sacramental preparation, RCIA, Alpha and CCO faith studies? While these settings can facilitate effective evangelization, they could generally be better. They can be more fruitful if people are trained and encouraged to evangelize one person at a time.

A NEW METHOD

Consider the words of St. John Paul II: "[E]vangelization will gain its full energy if it is a commitment, not to re-evangelize but to a New

Evangelization, new in its ardor, methods and expression ..." (Address to CELAM, March 9, 1983).

We acknowledge there are many ways to evangelize successfully. God is not limited by any given program or method. In today's ever-changing, highly secular society, methods that have worked in the past may no longer prove as effective. Indeed, we should be innovative, finding new methods to evangelize and new ways to express our timeless faith.

But we also shouldn't let the innovation distract us from recognizing what works or from relying on timeless truths about the human person. The fact is, there are concrete methods proven to be effective in evangelization.

The story of my encounter with Anne in Saskatoon, illustrated earlier in this chapter, presents an example of conversion occurring in the midst of an *intentional spiritual conversation*. When Anne and I were talking, we weren't just exploring a spiritual subject together for interest's sake. The ways I engaged in the conversation—the way I listened to her, the prayers I silently offered up, the words I picked and the questions I asked—were all aimed at better understanding her current spiritual state and helping her desire what God desired for her. I wanted to understand what she was seeing so I could help her understand what God sees for her.

Though seemingly simple and basic, this approach to evangelization is, I would argue, actually very deep and fundamental to our mission as Christians. It's also something frequently overlooked or omitted from our evangelical efforts in the Church. I would even go as far as saying that if we cannot engage in intentional spiritual conversations with our neighbours, we have not authentically embraced the call to mission, and none of our evangelical programming will bear fruit the way it could. But this is a bold claim, and requires explanation.

CONTEXT: "ONE PERSON AT A TIME"

True, authentic and fruitful evangelization is fundamentally relational. This may seem obvious, but, unfortunately, when evangelical principles are put into practice, it's easily lost in translation.

In proposing that Catholics engage in intentional spiritual conversations, I'm not simply making a utilitarian argument for a successful approach to evangelization. It's true that I've seen this approach bear fruit beyond my wildest expectations. But that's not the most important message for readers to take away. Much more important, in my view, is the fact that this approach reflects a Catholic understanding of the true dignity of each person. It reflects the fact that we're made for relationship (both with God and with one another), and that each soul is individually and infinitely precious to God. It invites us to see one another as God sees us and to share the Father's heart for each soul.

The person matters. It's only through personal, human connections that we gain insight into the beauty of individuals. It's how we find out what people are thinking, how they are feeling, what are they experiencing. In other words, my proposal that we adopt intentional spiritual conversations as the foundation of our evangelical efforts is as much a theological and anthropological argument as it is a practical one.

As a university student, I had a very memorable experience attending a friend's Christian youth group. As soon as I walked in, people came to greet me. Throughout the night, several people came up to me to find out who I was and asked about my story of faith. More than one person made sure to let me know that I was welcome to come back the next week. I was asked to leave my contact information and, to my surprise, I got a call the next day from the youth pastor himself! At first, I thought I must have made quite an impression for the pastor to take the time to call and invite me back. I eventually found out the reason he called me: new people like me were the focus of the group. I mattered, and the community made sure I knew that.

Sadly, I've had equally memorable experiences of the opposite approach. I began to reflect on my experience at the parish I attended while I was in university. I wondered if anyone in the parish community even knew I existed. What if I had gone to Sunday Mass, worshiped with them, left the church at the end of the service, been hit by a bus and died? And what if, on the following day, the local newspaper read, "University student dies after being struck by bus"? The parishioners and pastor might have read the newspaper and would be saddened by the tragedy. But I doubt they'd have had any idea I was part of their community. I felt like an insignificant part of a huge group that filled the church—as an individual, I did not matter. No one noticed whether I was there or not. The focus was on the crowd, not the person.

Such an impersonal approach makes it easy for someone to walk away. If we survey the crowd without connecting with individuals, we're in danger of making major faulty assumptions of a person's spiritual life based on their attendance or even involvement in Catholic ministries.

OUR RELATIONSHIP WITH CHRIST LEADS US TO OTHERS

Recall the power of Jesus' intimate, personal encounter with souls. When Nathaniel hears the Lord say, "I saw you under the fig tree" (John 1:48), he experiences the joy and awe of being known by Jesus, and exclaims, "Rabbi, you are the Son of God!" (John 1:49). Similarly, the Samaritan woman, following her profound encounter with Jesus at Jacob's well, "left her water jar and went back to the city" (John 4:28), telling everyone, "Come and see a man who told me everything I have ever done!" and, "He cannot be the Messiah, can he?" (John 4:29). For both these people, encountering Jesus, recognizing that he knows them personally and seeing that he cherishes them, leads them to worship Christ and to help others meet him.

As disciples of Christ, as Catholics who have said "yes" to the Lord's invitation to follow him, we too have experienced the power of an individual encounter with the Lord. Like the Samaritan woman, I can testify to the glory of a God who knows "everything I have ever done," who loves me and whose mercy never fails me. His love for me is *personal*: I'm not just one among a faceless multitude. I am his beloved.

Of course, when we accept that love, we are presented with Christ's "new commandment": "Just as I have loved you, you also should love one another" (John 13:34). We are to love one another with Christ's love. What does this mean for a missionary?

Just as conversion to Christ involves the recognition that Christ died for me, personally, and not just for "humanity" in an abstract sense, our missionary hearts ought to care about and desire the salvation of each person we meet. This means desiring to know them, to be with them, to understand their struggles and their hopes and to be open to the promptings of the Holy Spirit so that we can share the Gospel with them in love, trusting that God already knows them and has prepared their hearts to receive him:

> The missionary is convinced that, through the working of the Spirit, there already exists in individuals and peoples an expectation, even if an unconscious one, of knowing the truth about God, about man and about how we are to be set free from sin and death. The missionary's enthusiasm in proclaiming Christ comes from the conviction that he is responding to that expectation. *(Redemptoris Missio)*

Pope Francis, in his encyclical *Evangelii Gaudium*, emphasizes the significance of this kind of concrete personal accompaniment in the Church's missionary activity:

> In a culture paradoxically suffering from anonymity and at the same time obsessed with the details of other people's lives, shamelessly given over to morbid curiosity, *the Church must look more closely and sympathetically at others whenever necessary.* In our world, ordained ministers and other pastoral workers can *make present the fragrance of Christ's closeness and his personal gaze.* The Church will have to initiate everyone – priests, religious and laity – into this "art of accompaniment" which teaches us *to remove our sandals before the sacred ground of the other* (cf. Ex 3:5). (*Evangelii Gaudium*, emphasis added)

Each of us must be "initiated" into this "art of accompaniment," as Pope Francis puts it—an accompaniment which is personal, patient and loving, just as Christ's accompaniment is. Pope Francis even offers us a vision of what this might look like:

> Today, as the Church seeks to experience a profound missionary renewal, there is a kind of preaching which falls to each of us as a daily responsibility. It has to do with bringing the Gospel to the people we meet, whether they be our neighbours or complete strangers. This is the informal preaching which takes place in the middle of a conversation, something along the lines of what a missionary does when visiting a home. Being a disciple means being constantly ready to bring the love of Jesus to others, and this can happen unexpectedly and in any place: on the street, in a city square, during work, on a journey. *(Evangelii Gaudium)*

Consider that no one experienced a "trivial" encounter with Christ during his earthly life. In the same way, for the missionary disciple, each encounter with another person (whether family member, colleague or stranger on the bus) is sacred, an opportunity to respond to the Lord's call to love that individual with his salvific love. We recognize that "the love of Christ urges us" (2 Corinthians 5:14) to yearn for that person's eternal happiness:

> God created that person in his image, and he or she reflects something of God's glory. Every human being is the object of God's infinite tenderness, and he himself is present in their lives. Jesus offered his precious blood on the cross for that person. Appearances notwithstanding, every person is immensely holy and deserves our love. *(Evangelii Gaudium)*

In a world that is often hostile to Christ's message, this can be a hard truth to live by. For example, I was recently asked, "How do you speak to those people who are not interested or open to God and faith?" The questioner was suggesting that there are some people who are open, and there are others who are not. I pushed back on his premise, assuring him there is no one in the world who doesn't yearn for love, meaning, purpose, joy and freedom.

I know for certain that, whether they know it or not, every living soul is longing for a personal and life-changing encounter with the God who loves them. In the commonly used words of St. Augustine, "Our hearts are restless until they rest in thee" *(Confessions)*. St. John Paul II also dealt with this question in *Redemptoris Missio*:

> The missionary's enthusiasm for proclaiming Christ comes from the conviction that he is responding to [the person's innate expectation of knowing the truth about God, man and about how we are to be set free from sin and death], and so he does not become discouraged or cease his witness even when he is called to manifest his faith in an environment that is hostile or indifferent.

The question we need to ask ourselves is: Are we proposing God's love, or are we proposing devotions and doctrines?

I realize that all this, as reasonable as it might sound, may still seem a bit abstract. What does this mean, concretely, in terms of how one should approach intentional spiritual conversations? "Does it just mean talking about Jesus all the time?" someone might ask. "Surely it's more nuanced than that."

Let's delve into these questions. The next few sections of this book will be dedicated to explaining what I have in mind.

INTENTIONAL ACCOMPANIMENT: THE HEART AND SOUL OF EVANGELIZATION

One of the foundational tenets of CCO is "One person at a time." This means that our evangelization is focused on personal relationships. As a movement seeking to fulfill the Great Commission, that of making missionary disciples for Christ, we believe it's necessary that these relationships be about *intentionally accompanying* a person on their journey towards becoming a missionary disciple and growing in union with God. Because of how fundamental these ideas are to the thesis of this book, throughout this chapter I'll quote substantial sections of an internal document developed by CCO that deals with this subject.

Before defining *intentional accompaniment*, let's clarify what *accompaniment* means in this context:

> Accompaniment is walking alongside another on their pilgrimage to the Father. The pilgrimage is not your own; it is the pilgrimage of the one you accompany. The missionary cannot walk this pilgrimage for anyone. Each person must walk their own pilgrimage. However, the missionary can act as a guide along the way. Like a mountain climbing guide, the missionary has been through this journey before, and continues their own personal journey. Through the wisdom gleaned from their own guides and from experience, the missionary can help others navigate their pilgrimage. The missionary knows where to go to reach the goal, and so they can lead the pilgrim to their final destination, which is Christ himself. The missionary has not reached the final destination (i.e., heaven), nor have they achieved perfection in their own pilgrimage. They are, however, further along the path and that means that they can guide new pilgrims who are just starting their pilgrimage. As the missionary continues further down the pilgrimage route, they can continue to direct pilgrims along the paths they have already travelled. ("Intentional Accompaniment")

This definition helps clarify a few key points. Each person, we understand, must make their own journey; no one else can make it for them. That being said, the missionary disciple can supply the guidance, knowledge and encouragement they've gained from their own spiritual journey to help another pilgrim on their way to Christ. It is not that the missionary disciple is already a saint or someone in perfect union with God; rather, they've simply travelled this part of the journey before, and can put their wisdom and experience at the service of another.

As an addendum to this, it's worth recalling that the missionary disciple is not the one leading the pilgrimage:

> The goal is not for the pilgrim to follow the missionary. Christ himself is the leader on the pilgrimage of discipleship and, therefore, the goal of the pilgrim is to follow Christ. They are to become a disciple of Christ, not a disciple of their missionary guide. The missionary must always keep the pilgrim focused on Christ. As *Evangelii Gaudium* states, "Spiritual accompaniment must lead others ever closer to God, in whom we attain true freedom" *(Evangelii Gaudium)*. ("Intentional Accompaniment")

What, then, do we mean by "intentional accompaniment"?

> In one of his post-Resurrection appearances, Jesus commissioned his Apostles to share in his ministry to the world: "As the Father has sent me, so I send you" (John 20:21). The Church therefore shares in Christ's ministry to reconcile the world to the Father. It is Christ who has accomplished this reconciliation, but he invites us to be a part of the mission to make disciples of all nations (cf. Matthew 28:19-20), which we accomplish through Accompaniment. *However, this accompaniment should not be aimless.* When Jesus invites the Apostles into his ministry in the Great Commission, he specifically commands them to *make* disciples. To make something requires an intention and a plan. This is why we refer to our ministry specifically as *Intentional Accompaniment*. The role of the missionary is to engage in Prophetic Listening, putting together a strategic plan to incarnate the Lord's prophetic vision for the individual.

> Of course, one cannot make a disciple on their own; it is a work of the Holy Spirit in both the individual and the missionary. However, the multiplying missionary cannot simply walk alongside someone and hope they become a disciple of Christ. The multiplying missionary must have an intentional plan of how to make a disciple, and ultimately a multiplying missionary. ("Intentional Accompaniment")

Again, there are several key points to draw from this explanation. We understand that reconciliation with God has been achieved through Christ, and that conversion is ultimately the work of the Holy Spirit. At the same time, we accept the commission that Christ gave us to "make disciples of all nations," a call to deliberate action and intentionality. Christ desires our "yes" to the call to mission, just as he awaits our "yes" to his saving love.

In light of this, we need to resist, on the one hand, the temptation to imagine the work of salvation depends entirely on our own efforts as missionaries and, on the other, the temptation to take a passive attitude towards evangelization, imagining that God would never ask for deliberate, intentional cooperation from us to fulfill his plans. We need to offer authentic friendship to the people in our lives, but also investigate the lay of the land. We should look for signs of where a person is on their journey to Christ, asking the Holy Spirit to show us how to help them take the next step forward in their spiritual journey, while never losing sight of the ultimate goal of spiritual accompaniment, which is union with Christ. We need to share the Lord's dream for each person.

As an aside: Certainly people in our lives can and do come to God despite our lack of particular attention to their souls. Still, it would be dangerously presumptuous to "opt out" of the call to mission on these grounds. Indeed, our God is a miracle-worker and a prodigiously loving Father, not limited by the response of his children; however, we should consider that a person's un-looked-for conversion may be the fruit of a seed sown by someone else, long ago, or of graces won by another missionary's suffering, prayer and sacrifice, perhaps in another time or place. God asks for our assent to his plan, and his plan is to spread the Gospel through his disciples.

CCO's document on intentional accompaniment provides this helpful analogy:

> Consider a gardening analogy: A seed has all the potential it needs to grow into what is meant to be; it just needs the right environment. A gardener intentionally plants the seed in fertile ground, and in a place where it will get sun; he waters it; he weeds around it. He needs to continually evaluate what can be done to provide an optimal environment for that plant to thrive. However, the gardener

does not provide the actual growth. In a similar way, our role as Multiplying Missionaries is to provide an environment and intentionally create conditions for people to grow into Multiplying Missionaries. Through the Holy Spirit, each individual already has all the potential to become a Multiplying Missionary, and the Holy Spirit will be the one who gives the needed graces to activate this potential. The missionary's job is to support the work of the Holy Spirit by trying to provide the best environment for growth. We do this by engaging in Prophetic Listening, being attentive to the Holy Spirit's plans for the individual and responding to the Spirit's promptings by creating intentional plans to help foster their spiritual growth. This plan is carried out in the context of a relationship of Intentional Accompaniment. ("Intentional Accompaniment.")

We also need to emphasize, however, that this model emphatically rejects the idea of turning human relationships into "projects":

At the heart of all Intentional Accompaniment is relationship. As St. Paul wrote, "So deeply do we care for you that we are determined to share with you not only the gospel of God but also our own selves, because you have become very dear to us" (2 Thessalonians 2:8). Without genuine relationships of trust, we risk our Intentional Accompaniment becoming a task to be completed, and people may become goals to be accomplished rather than brothers and sisters with transcendent dignity. It is on the basis of relationships of trust that we may be granted the privilege of having influence in the life of someone else, and through this influence be granted the opportunity to Intentionally Accompany them on their pilgrimage to the Father. ("Intentional Accompaniment")

In other words, we're called to cherish the relationships God has entrusted to us, caring for each person the way Christ cares for them. We "rejoice with those who rejoice, weep with those who weep" (Romans 12:15), experiencing genuine compassion and concern for them, even apart from their current openness or lack of openness to Christ. A more detailed explanation of this attitude is helpful:

We should never befriend someone simply with the ulterior motive to evangelize. The missionary should always be seeking to build loving, genuine relationships that are based in the personal care for another.

At the same time, we know that the most loving thing that we can do for another is to introduce them to Christ, who can bring them ultimate fulfillment and happiness in this life and the next. Our love for others should therefore compel us to want to share the Gospel with them.

Our Witnessing is therefore two-fold. We want to build solid friendships with others first and foremost for the sake of good friendships. As these relationships develop, we should always be mindful to be offering an inviting and contagious witness to the faith that might help our friend begin to develop a curiosity towards the faith. *It is important to note that the speed at which these relationships will grow will vary. It may take five minutes or five years to establish a relationship of trust.* Prophetic Listening will help us to determine how quickly the relationship is progressing. ("Intentional Accompaniment")

While patience and faithfulness in developing trust are invaluable, and a fruit of genuine love, I want to re-emphasize part of this message: sometimes trust develops very quickly. Indeed, there are likely many relationships in our lives where that trust already exists. In the Church, we often talk about people today (whether baptized or not) seeming uninterested in or closed to the Gospel, perhaps because they haven't overtly expressed religious curiosity. I'd argue that many of these people likely *are* open, and may even be curious about our faith, but are waiting for us to make the "first move" in terms of talking about the Gospel.

Are we sufficiently aware of these opportunities? I suspect we underestimate the frequency with which God invites us to share the reason for our hope. Again, however, we must be sensitive to the promptings of the Holy Spirit, and gauge the level of trust in any relationship. In extreme cases, it may be years before a person is willing even to listen to an explanation of who Jesus is. Genuine love trusts that those years of friendship are never wasted.

When we engage in prophetic listening—that is, prayerful listening to the way a person talks about themselves, God and the world, asking the Holy Spirit to help us understand where that person is on their spiritual journey—it's helpful to have a roadmap for gauging where the person is in relation to God's purpose for them (which is nothing less than perfect union with Christ in heaven). In CCO, we use a framework developed from our own initial models of discipleship and from Sherry Weddell's "Five Thresholds of Conversion," outlined in her important book, *Form-*

ing Intentional Disciples. The purpose of any such framework is to understand a person's relationship with Christ, and to have a clear sense of what the "next step" of discipleship might be for them in order to help them reach it. As our intentional accompaniment document explains,

> ... the goal of Intentional Accompaniment is to help people encounter Jesus Christ and assist their growth in holiness and mission. However, like any good first responder, before we can help anyone, we must assess the situation. It would be unwise for a paramedic to treat someone's high blood pressure before dealing with the gaping wound on the patient's head. Similarly, it is unproductive for missionaries to train someone to share the Gospel if this person has not accepted Jesus as his or her saviour. We must assess spiritual situations in order to best help people in their spiritual growth.

Could we describe in simple terms where a given person stands in relation to Christ? Is the person among "the Lost" (not to be confused with "the damned")—in other words, those who haven't met Christ nor made any decision to approach him? As missionaries, our attitude towards the Lost is critical: "Having a heart for the Lost is a crucial mind-set for any missionary. Our desire is for all people to have the opportunity to encounter Christ and become his disciple" ("Intentional Accompaniment"). Such a person may not yet be willing to listen to the Gospel message. They may completely lack trust in Christians or the Catholic Church. Reaching out in authentic love to help build that trust might be our primary calling in many encounters, as missionaries:

> [T]he first stage in any person's journey to faith begins with trust. The Lost often do not have any relationship of trust with the Church, and so finding even one individual within the Church whom they can trust is a step in the right direction. We must make the personal investment in relationships so that we can be that person within the Church that others trust. ("Intentional Accompaniment")

Once a foundation of trust exists, a person might become curious about our faith, though they may not yet be ready to consider it as a real option for themselves. In all these initial stages, the primary mode of our intentional accompaniment will likely be that of witnessing to the goodness of the faith through our loving actions. We may not yet have the chance to proclaim the Gospel in clear terms.

The task of proclamation is key, however. We should always be willing to gauge a person's openness to the *kerygma*. Again, some people who *are* open may not be bold enough to ask us, and even those who are actively seeking God may assume we'll take the initiative to share our faith.

> As we build relationships, whether quickly or over extended periods of time, we should expect that our witness of life will provide opportunities for the procla-mation of the *kerygma*. We should expect these opportunities to arise as we see individuals grow from spiritual curiosity to a spiritual openness and seeking. As this shift occurs, the individual we are accompanying will begin to demonstrate more openness to spiritual matters, and may even show interest in small levels of commitment in this search, such as joining a Faith Study or an Alpha program. These, and many others, can be indicators that we have established a relation-ship of trust that gives us the opportunity to proclaim the Gospel in a clear and simple way. Our primary mode of action then shifts to an active proclamation of the Gospel. Here we will intentionally seek opportunities to have spiritual con-versations with the intention of introducing others to the person of Jesus through the proclamation of the *kerygma*. ("Intentional Accompaniment")

Recall our discussion of initial conversion in earlier sections of this book. We want the person to have a clear sense of their own relation-ship with God and be able to express their response to the Gospel:

> When a person chooses to become a disciple, they have begun the process of discipleship: their pilgrimage of following Christ, growing in maturity in holiness and mission. After all, a disciple is "one who accepts and assists in spreading the doctrines of another" (Merriam-Webster Dictionary). To accept the doctrine of an-other requires a deliberate decision; you cannot be forced to accept the doctrine of another. Therefore, you cannot become a disciple by accident; it is always a choice. Since it is a choice, we can work to pinpoint when this choice was made. The choice may have been in a particular moment, or it may have been over a period of time, but if one is a disciple, there is a choice that was made at some point along the way that brought that person to the decision to begin living as a disciple. ("Intentional Accompaniment")

CCO uses "relationship diagrams" to help people understand and ex-press their relationship with God. (More on these in a later section of this book.) The advantage of these diagrams is that they don't require the missionary to tell the person what to do; they let the person discover the state of their relationship with God and then express the desire of their heart. They also allow the missionary to see what kind of accompaniment they ought to provide. If the person does not yet see Christ as the centre of their life, the missionary's primary task may be to proclaim the *kerygma* and invite the person to respond. Once the person *can* clearly affirm that Christ is at the centre of their life, the goal of the missionary disciple is to help them grow in holiness and commitment to mission, with both parties journeying ever closer to Christ. In other words, even when we see that a person has made a wholehearted "yes" to the invitation of the Gospel, the work of accompaniment isn't over—our aim is not just to help that person experience an initial conversion, but to accompany them in their growth as disciples of Christ.

While the focus of this book is primarily on proclaiming the *kerygma* and accompanying someone through their initial conversion, it's worth touching on what we mean by the call to make missionary disciples, or "multiplying missionaries," as CCO usually puts it:

> Multiplication can be summarized as the invitation to Missionary Formation. The goal of Multiplication is to build a disciple into one who is ready to make disciples themselves. It follows St. Paul's ministry model from 2 Timothy 2:2: "And what you have heard from me through many witnesses entrust to faithful people who will be able to teach others as well."

> All disciples of Christ are called to grow in holiness, the call to become more conformed to Christ in our heart, mind, soul, and actions, and to the mission of evangelization, making disciples of all nations (cf. Mt 28:19-20). The role of the Multiplying Missionary is to multiply the attitudes, skills, and knowledge they have acquired in their discipleship pilgrimage with those they are ministering to. They are intentionally accompanying disciples on their pilgrimage towards maturity in holiness and mission. ("Intentional Accompaniment")

Helping someone make an initial response to the Gospel is one of our tasks as evangelists, but God's desire—and hence, ours—for each person goes beyond that. Even from a merely practical perspective, consider that I can never reach each person on my own. If every person who read this book shared the *kerygma* with every person they knew, we'd still reach only a tiny fraction of humanity. On the other hand, if the person I accompany receives the same love for Christ and his people that I have, and desires to go out and help others experience that love so as to be able to pass it on, we can dare to hope that the message of the Gospel really could spread throughout the whole world.

As CCO sees it,

> ... Intentional Accompaniment is the framework in which all ministry is accomplished. Whether it is in meeting someone for the first time, or meeting a long-time member of your ministry who is seeking to grow in maturity, the mindset of a Multiplying Missionary is to walk alongside another person as they walk on their pilgrimage towards the relationship with God that they have been created for. The Missionary not only walks alongside, but acts as a guide who has an intentional plan to bring a person to conversion or, after conversion, to an ever-deepening experience of discipleship which leads to maturity in holiness and mission. This is the call that Jesus gave to all his disciples at the Ascension when he commanded his disciples to go out and "make disciples of all nations".

> Robert Coleman provides an apt summary of the importance of this ministry of Intentional Accompaniment:

> "His [Jesus] whole evangelistic strategy—indeed, the fulfillment of his very purpose for coming into the world, dying on the cross, and rising from the grave—depended on the faithfulness of his chosen disciples to this task. It did not matter how small the group was to start with so long as they reproduced and taught their disciples to reproduce. This was the way his Church was to win—through the dedicated lives of those who knew the Savior so well that his Spirit and method constrained them to tell others. As simple as it may seem, this was the way the gospel would conquer. He had no other plan." (Robert Coleman, *The Master Plan of Evangelism, 2nd Edition*, p. 102) ("Intentional Accompaniment")

THE FIRST STEP OF AN INTENTIONAL SPIRITUAL CONVERSATION: PRAY

As I've already noted, we need to be prepared to have *intentional spiritual conversations* with the people in our lives. By this, I mean authentic conversations in which the missionary listens and speaks from a desire to accompany a person on a pilgrimage ever closer to Christ—or more immediately, to help them reach a new threshold of discipleship, such as curiosity about the Catholic faith, initial conversion to Christ or greater maturity as a multiplying missionary. This is our intention for others because it is Christ's loving intention for each person: The love of Christ compels us to share his goodness with those we encounter, trusting that we are cooperating with grace that goes ahead of us.

Before we begin any evangelical initiative, however, we need to start with prayer to the Holy Spirit. We are about to engage in a conversation where we invite a person into spiritual realities. The Holy Spirit is the principal agent of evangelization, and we need Him to enable them to "make this act of faith … the grace of God and the interior help of the Holy Spirit must precede and assist, moving the heart …" *(Dei Verbum)* So, wherever this conversation occurs, we can ask for the Holy Spirit to be present with us and to move in the heart of the person we'll be speaking with.

It's good to integrate this kind of prayer in our daily prayer lives, even if we don't yet see the opportunity to share the Gospel with someone. We can ask the Lord to prepare the way, to soften hearts, to let us see what the Lord sees and to help us be discerning yet courageous in how we speak. On the other hand, the opportunity to share the Gospel can sometimes arise suddenly or unexpectedly. In such a case, we can pray silently to the Holy Spirit as we listen to the person speak.

THE FUNDAMENTAL IMPORTANCE OF LISTENING

While clear and simple kerygmatic proclamation is critical (and desperately needed in the Church), I want to pause before discussing a method of presenting the *kerygma* to emphasize a point that might otherwise be overlooked. This point is that the main role of the missionary during an intentional spiritual conversation should almost always be less that of a *speaker* than it is that of a *listener.*

Recall that the invitation of the Gospel is profoundly personal. While a straightforward kerygmatic proclamation has real power to reach people, regardless of their cultural context, age or education, we should always be looking for the ways in which the message of the Gospel fits into a person's particular circumstances. We trust that it always does. We seek opportunities to help a person recognize that their deepest desire is for Christ. We probably won't be able to do this, however, if we don't first listen to what a person has to say.

When I engage in an intentional spiritual conversation with someone, I am primarily focused on listening and asking questions. My goal is not to speak a lot, but only to say the words or ask the questions that will help the person reflect with greater clarity on the state of their own soul and express a desire to move closer to God. The fact is, I don't *know* the state of that person's soul, so I can't presume to tell them what it is. But if, instead, I listen with sincere attention and ask the person to explain or elaborate on things they say about themselves and God, or if I ask them to share their reaction to a situation we observe, a moment in their lives, or a spiritual idea, I get a much clearer sense of who Christ is to them—as do they. I can then frame the initial proclamation of the Gospel in terms that make sense to them, responding to their own questions and desires, and they can perceive the relevance of the proclamation without my having to prove it to them.

This is something that I can only accomplish in the context of a personal relationship based on trust. (Again, we shouldn't underestimate how quickly sufficient trust can develop. This is where we need to listen carefully to both the person we're accompanying and to the promptings of the Holy Spirit.) It's in such a context that intentional spiritual conversations play out, and it's in this context that we are typically best able to invite people to respond to Christ's personal, saving love, reflecting his love in our own love for the person in front of us.

As an example, I remember speaking with a self-described practicing Catholic who assured me he loved God and the Church. However, after listening to him talk about many things and seeing how he was living his life, it was my impression that he'd never experienced a personal relationship with Jesus Christ. As he launched into a rant about how the world was wrong on so many issues and the Church was right, I heard him make a passing remark suggesting God likely didn't know or care about his insignificant life the way He cared about the state of the world.

The statement, "God doesn't care much about my insignificant life," was worth clarifying. I asked him what he meant. I listened as he shared how he believed strongly in God, but had never had any real encounter with Him. It was not me making a judgment based on my impression; rather, it was him answering the question and confronting the present state of his relationship with Jesus. Based on this knowledge, the door was open for me to ask, "Do you want to know Jesus Christ in a personal way?" This question invited him again to reflect on whether he desired to have a renewed relationship with Jesus. I could respond based on his desire for intimacy with Christ rather than my own assumptions.

Similarly, another friend admitted to me he was going through a difficult time and expressed how overwhelmed he was. I shared with him how, when I was in a similar situation, my faith helped me through it. This led me to ask him, "Have you ever considered turning to God for help?" His response was, "I don't believe in God or in the Church anymore."

As evangelists, we need to respect that many of our people haven't had a positive experience of Church. Indeed, I needed to allow an honest conversation about his views and his experience of faith and Church. I listened to him earnestly, empathizing with his experiences and concerns. At a certain point in the conversation, I saw another opportunity to share with him how I still found my faith to be relevant and life-giving, and as he seemed open to hearing about it, I told him. He left the conversation feeling better about his situation, respecting how faith was important and helpful in my life but not yet seeing the need to turn to God in his life.

A year later, I got together with this same friend in a coffee shop. He shared with me that he had gone back to Church. I asked him a lot of questions about why he did it and what his experience had been coming back. Based on what he shared with me, I saw it was the right time to share the *kerygma* with him. He responded gratefully to it. It was a beautiful moment of conversion.

What is needed in intentional accompaniment is the art of asking questions: listening attentively to what's being said, and being ready to ask follow-up questions. This is the only way we'll be able share with another person what they need to hear—what God wants them to hear—and not just what we want to tell them.

CHAPTER 3:
SHARING THE *KERYGMA*—
AN ADAPTABLE MODEL FROM CCO

In 1988, CCO committed itself to reaching out to the millions of Catholics who had wandered away from the Church. The challenge was figuring out how to bridge the gap so these souls could return home. The most common approach people were taking at the time was to invite a lapsed Catholic to Mass, telling them to try to pray or to observe some devotion or other. But as people tried this, the exodus of young people continued. It wasn't working.

We searched for new methods, with some of our biggest breakthroughs coming through trial and error. We asked ourselves endless questions. *What are students really asking? What don't they know? What are the common barriers to conversion?* This led us to develop a systematic presentation of the *kerygma* that was intended not to impose the faith, but to propose it in all its beauty and power.

I want to share this method of presenting the *kerygma*, not because I think everyone should evangelize exactly the way CCO does, but because I want to provide a concrete, adaptable example of how to share the Gospel, which is often lacking in Catholic ministries. Indeed, we've found this way of sharing the Gospel has helped countless people recognize what God is calling them to, allowing them the freedom to give an authentic "yes" to Christ.

That being said, it's not the specifics of the materials or phrasing that I'm advocating, but that Catholic missionaries would share God's heart for each person, be bold in their proclamation and invitation and be equipped to share the *kerygma* simply and clearly. For a person hearing the Gospel to make a radical assent of the will and intellect, they need to be clear on what they are assenting to. It is our responsibility to let them know, with clarity and simplicity, what the Church proposes as the way to salvation.

I was tested in this in a very personal context when one of my children came to Angele and me in a crisis of faith. We did not just encourage him to trust in God, to pray or to go to Mass. (Such responses, however well-intended, may only lead to more questions and doubt.) What our son needed from us was the full content of the Gospel, with an invitation to a full commitment. As we explained God's love for him and how that love was shown through the life, death and resurrection of Jesus, there was no ambiguity or vagueness in our proclamation.

Our son saw he needed to respond with a "yes," and through our testimony, he knew to expect that his "yes" would deal with his crisis of faith. Not long after our conversation, he was on the bus and, sitting there, gave the *kerygma* his full consideration. Silently, on that bus, he placed Christ at the centre of his life. (Truly, conversion can happen anywhere.)

He did not see heaven open up. Nor did he feel overwhelmed by God's presence. It was quite uneventful, really. That doesn't matter. If we look beyond the sentiment, we see a young man who made a life-changing decision to live no longer for himself but for God. Later, he had other significant moments of encounter, but that bus ride remains the milestone marker of when he found himself on the right path.

I know my son isn't the only person whose "yes" was facilitated by a clear proclamation of the *kerygma*—far from it. My desire is that all Catholic evangelists would be able to share the message with those who need to hear it. I hope CCO's four-point proclamation will be helpful to readers in this respect.

A FOUR-POINT MESSAGE

In CCO, we've simplified the *kerygma* using four points communicated in a systematic way. We begin by explaining the purpose of creation, speaking of God's love and His desire to be in a personal relationship with each of us. The second truth we present is the "fall of man." This is all about sin as the fundamental factor keeping us from experiencing God's personal love. This leads to the third truth, which introduces Jesus as the second person of the Trinity, the one who came to restore this relationship between us and God. At this point, we've communicated what God has done for us. The remaining point is "redemption," an invitation for us to respond by letting Jesus Christ redeem us for eternal communion with God.

FIRST POINT: GOD'S LOVE

The most appropriate place to begin is where the Catechism begins (see *Catechism of the Catholic Church*, Prologue)—with God's love for us and his desire for us to know and love him.

How often have we heard that "God is love" and "He loves us"? However inspiring these messages may seem to us, they can sound trite if they're not communicated properly. That's why, when we speak about God's love and being part of the Church, it should be in the context of a relationship which speaks of the fundamental nature of God: the Father, the Son and the Holy Spirit. That is an active relationship of unitive love. Love is more incarnate and tangible in the context of a relationship.

When we speak of God's desire for a "relationship" with us, we catch people's attention. Humans are all about relationships: they're what we do, how we function and what we desire in our lives. We can all relate to building new relationships or restoring broken ones. If, at the heart of the Christian message, it is God's desire to be in a dynamic and intimate relationship with us, then we can attract the attention of the person in front of us, no matter how far away or antagonistic they may be towards the Church.

I can't emphasize the importance of the personal nature of God's love strongly enough. The cruciality of this message hit home when I invited a young Catholic man—let's call him Tom—to be in a *Discovery* faith study. Tom was struggling with his faith and openly stated he no longer believed that God existed. At one point during the study, I asked the participants, "Who believes God loves them?" Tom quickly raised his hand, saying, "Yes, I believe that God loves me." When I asked him why he so quickly put up his hand, especially in light of not believing God exists, he explained that he grew up always being told that God loves him. After further reflection, he continued, "I always understood God's love, but I never experienced it in my life. It seemed to elude me. I guess I don't really believe God is love."

Based on countless testimonies of Catholics who speak of their faith before conversion, this is a common reality. We observe this in the indifference of many people who go to Church each Sunday and the great number of baptized Catholics who have wandered away from the Church. Surely, if they had an experience of God's great love for them, they would act differently.

So how do we go beyond simply stating the truth of God's love to connect love with a personal relationship? The difference is that the former is merely a statement of an idea, while the latter implies an invitation to respond personally to that love. The true nature of love cannot be expressed by a static intellectual statement of belief; it's dynamic. Love's intention is to reach deep into our lives, piercing our very being. Love is passionate; it is intimate. Love brings joy and fulfillment. Love is experiential; we feel it, we know it, it changes us. When we are in love, we cannot say, "Love eludes me," because it changes everything.

We present this foundation of God's love to somebody with the hope that they would know and experience God in this way. To do that, we need to communicate that the nature of God's love is personal and directed towards each individual. This may seem obvious, but the common understanding is that "God loves everyone." It's true that God loves all of humanity. But more precisely, we want to communicate that God loves each person uniquely. He knows each of us by name.

Imagine the following scenario as an illustration. I come into a room full of people and say, "I love you all." Maybe some people in the room would think, "OK, I think I believe André," moved to believe I was talking about them. But I suspect most of the crowd wouldn't really take it personally. It may sound nice, but most would conclude, "He's not really talking to me." It'd be easy for them to walk away, indifferent, unchanged by my statement of love. Is this not what most of our people experience when somebody tells us that God loves us?

However, it would be a whole different response if I walked down into the crowd to a particular person and pronounced, specifically, my unfailing love for them. That person could no longer be indifferent or unaffected by the words of love. They could no longer say, "Oh, he's not talking about me." They couldn't leave thinking nothing has changed. That would be absurd! Instead, they would face a choice to receive, accept and respond to this love, or to reject it and walk away. There would be no room for ambivalence.

When love is directed towards a person, when God says, "I love you," a person can't help but notice.

THE BRIDGE ANALOGY, PART 1

Through CCO's experience in evangelization, we've found that providing analogies and visual aids can help someone understand the Gospel message more clearly. Throughout the discussion of presenting the *kerygma* in this book, I'll share a tool we call the "bridge analogy." It's based on an analogy used by St. Catherine of Sienna to explain our need for Christ.

Here's how to share the first point of the *kerygma* using the bridge analogy. Grab a piece of paper or whatever else is at hand; if you're in a coffee shop, a napkin works just as well. Draw this illustration:

STAGE 1

God
HEAVEN

Humanity
EARTH

© 2011 Catholic Christian Outreach

St. Catherine of Siena talks about how Adam and Eve were created in the image of God. They experienced communion with God and would have continued to grow in that relationship. As you're explaining this to the person in front of you, let them know that God wants a relationship with them, too. This is a great chance to share your own experience with God's personal love.

You can also go to the Scriptures—like the first chapters of Genesis—to show how this is true. Consider reading the story of the creation of Man and reflecting on God's original intention for his creation. After all, we know the Word of God has the power to convert (see Romans 1:16) and is "living and active" (Hebrews 4:12).

Next, ask the person you're speaking to, "Do you perceive God in a personal way?"

SECOND POINT: INTRODUCING SIN AND SEPARATION

If somebody isn't familiar with the idea of God's personal love, it can naturally inspire questions: "Why don't I experience this love?" or, "How can I experience this love?" Unfortunately, the answer is a difficult one to hear: our relationship with God is broken because of sin. It is crucial to communicate this truth without being judgmental—simply state it as a fact.

Sin is a concept that often confuses people. Sometimes it's tempting to avoid talking about it altogether. But we should seize the opportunity to clarify common misconceptions about sin, and emphasize the truth: sin is anything we do that negatively affects our relationships with other people and with God.

I recognize there are those in the Church who have been wounded by a disproportionate emphasis on sin. I grieve the effects of these wounds, and I grieve for the souls who haven't seen God's love and mercy witnessed through the Church. That being said, we make a mistake just as serious if we refuse to talk about sin. I want to emphasize this here, as there are undoubtedly readers hoping for a "shortcut" to sharing the Gospel without having to address this potentially difficult topic.

The fact is, just as an emphasis on sin is harsh and fruitless apart from a witness to God's infinite mercy, a celebration of God's saving grace is meaningless if there is nothing serious we need to be saved *from*. If I hope to be able to explain who Christ is, I need the person to understand that our relationship with God has been broken by sin in a profound way. I want the person to recognize their own profound need for a loving saviour.

Given the reservations and fears some readers might have on this topic, I'll elaborate on some points that might help us in our proclamation of the Gospel.

ORIGINAL SIN

An explanation of the concept of original sin helps our understanding of the Gospel. When God created us, it was not His intention that we would sin and be separated from him for eternity. He didn't intend for us to experience physical and spiritual death. God's intention, motivated by love, was for us to have continuous unity with Him. He made this possible for our first parents—Adam and Eve—by infusing them with supernatural graces: sanctifying grace, original justice. These are theological phrases that simply mean Adam and Eve were given the capacity to share the life of God and not die. They were also given the grace to live differently, with the gifts of understanding, knowledge and the mysteries of life. They had the grace to control their desires, and the ability to choose love instead of lust.

These gifts enable humans, beginning with Adam and Eve, to be in right relationship with God, with each other and with all of creation. And there's another gift that was essential for them, and for all of us to embrace God's love: the gift of free will. The freedom to choose.

In Genesis, the reality of free will is manifested in the tree in the middle of the garden. God told Adam to enjoy everything around him and to freely eat of every tree of the garden except for the tree in the middle of garden. Why do you think God did that? Why do you think He placed it in the garden only to tell Adam that he couldn't even touch it, never mind eat its fruit? Most people see this tree as a kind of a trap, as though God is trying to trick us. Maybe it seems as if God is saying, "I'm going to see if they go for it. Then I'm going to punish them and prove they need me." Surely a tree like that couldn't come from a loving God. But that's not the meaning of the tree. The tree offers free will. It's an expression of love.

We understand that love cannot be forced. Without the possibility of rejecting an offer of relationship, a "yes" to that relationship is meaningless. (Recall everything we discussed earlier about freedom and consent with respect to conversion.) If there is no real possibility of saying "no," neither is there any context for a true "yes."

God desired an authentic "yes" from His first children (as he does from us). He told them how to live in right relationship with Him. He gave them everything they needed to do so, and provided the "boundaries" and rules for that relationship so that, informed by their intellects and motivated by a desire for relationship with God, they could choose to live as they were created to live.

But God would not prevent them from overstepping those boundaries if they willed to overstep them. As beings made in His image, they were the only part of His earthly creation with such radical freedom. They were free to say "no" to God, to reject the loving plan of the one who made them. God warned Adam and Eve that this "no" would be a destructive choice. They had been created for life—for life in God—and turning away from that life by rejecting Him meant choosing physical and spiritual death. Still, God had created them as beings with free will, able to reject the love they were made for. Only by allowing humans this freedom, reflective of their dignity, could there exist the meaningful possibility of their *choosing* to remain in right relationship with God, allowing for authentic love between God and His people, an image of God's eternal, overflowing Trinitarian love.

But we know how things turned out. Adam and Eve chose to not trust in God. They chose not to live within the boundaries of the relationship, and when they broke those boundaries, they broke the relationship. They thought it would be better to live differently, to disobey God, and the consequences were eternal. It broke the relationship between God and man. The supernatural graces God had given them were taken away. They had been able to share the very life of God, but now they were left on their own.

This might seem harsh, but it was the result of perfect justice. Man decided to reject the life he was made for and had to face the consequences of that decision.

CONCUPISCENCE: SIN IN OUR OWN LIVES

Humans have a natural tendency to sin. It's what we call *concupiscence*, and it entered the world when Adam and Even crossed the boundaries that God had set for them. Before that, they had been inclined toward God and goodness, but their sin shifted their inclination towards sin. And this inclination persists throughout humanity—you, me … everybody.

It affects each of us individually, and that's important to explain. But as we explain sin to someone, we also need to be sensitive and make sure they don't feel we're judging or criticizing them. The tendency to sin is a reality of the human condition. That being said, we can't simply blame Adam and Eve. We recognize that we, too, have freedom, and we, too, use it to make destructive choices.

When we love in a less than perfect way, that's sin. We quickly fall into this state when we wake up each morning: we fail to sacrifice for others, we think uncharitable thoughts, we take the selfish route. We are all sinners. Even though this sin is widespread, we can't fall into the trap of thinking of sin as a casual mistake. It has eternal consequences. We find ourselves in a broken relationship with God. And that's a disheartening place to be.

The message of sin is sensitive to communicate, but I've done just that with thousands of university students over the years. Mercifully, instead of feeling judged or offended by what I said, they've related to it. Sin doesn't mean we're fundamentally evil beings—after all, God created us in his own image and saw that we were "very good." But it's a real and serious problem, all the same. We all know, if we look honestly at our lives, that we've done things we know were wrong. We've hurt other people.

You can expect a similar response when you start a discussion of sin: an appreciation that human choices and behaviour are at the heart of our spiritual problem. It's not that we've annoyed God and He's no longer interested in us. It's that we've done something to break the relationship. We understand how this works from the dynamics of human relationships. They require care, engagement and sacrifice—a giving of ourselves. We only experience the richness of love when we offer ourselves to it. We have to engage with it, without any presumptions. The same thing applies to our relationship with God. Our care for this relationship determines the sort of intimacy we experience with God. How we treat God is going to affect how close we are to Him.

SEEING SIN HELPS US SEE GOD'S MERCY

St. Augustine teaches us another reason not to avoid talking about sin. He stresses in *Confessions* that being mindful of how far we have fallen enables us to discover God's relentless and abundant mercies. St. Augustine brings to mind his "past foulness, and the carnal corruptions of [his] soul," not out of love for these vanities, but recounts them as a reminder of the open door that leads to a love of God. The saint reveals an important truth: the search for God begins when we start to understand ourselves. Understanding ourselves can only happen in reference to God. It's in light of God's great mercy that we can honestly reflect on our doubts, struggles, fears, weakness and pride.

THE BRIDGE ANALOGY, PART 2

With this understanding, let us now go back to the bridge analogy illustration and to Adam and Eve. If you have a Bible, go to Genesis, chapter 3 and read through it with your friend. To connect Adam and Eve's decision to turn away from God with the effect of that decision, write the word "sin" horizontally between God and man. Genesis says that our first parents were cast out of the garden, which suggests separation between man and God. For effect, draw a river, as seen in the image below, showing the separation. Explain that the river is deep and powerful; it's impossible to cross by our own efforts. Write down the word "separation": this is what happens in human relationships when we don't care for the other. However, this separation from God and his love is grave. It's eternal.

Explain how in Romans 6 we read that the consequence of our sin is also death. (Again, if you have your Bible with you, and if time permits, reading the relevant Scripture passage might be helpful.) Write the word "death" as illustrated below. Spiritual death is for eternity. I suggest that you go over the illustration again and emphasize the consequences of our sin as much as you can.

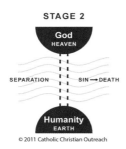

Give the person time to ponder this upsetting picture so they can comprehend the seriousness of the situation, then ask them how they feel about it.

The point of this illustration is to bring somebody to ask, "Is this true in my life?" and then to realize it is indeed true—and relevant to them. If you sense the person comprehends humanity is sinful but isn't relating to it personally, the "lifeguard analogy" can be helpful.

THE LIFEGUARD ANALOGY: A FURTHER ANALOGY TO HELP COMMUNICATE OUR NEED FOR A SAVIOUR

When I go to the beach, I recognize and respect the importance of having a lifeguard on duty. The lifeguard is there to help those in need … but I don't feel like I'm one of those people. I'm a competent swimmer. When I swim, I wave to acknowledge him and head to the deep waters. That's the extent of our relationship.

But what happens if I need him, after all? One day, as I'm swimming, I unexpectedly swallow a mouthful of water and begin to choke. Gasping for air, I swallow more water. I begin to panic as I start to sink. My head goes under the surface once, twice. At this point, I'm certain if I'm submerged a third time, I will die.

Here, my attitude towards the lifeguard has changed drastically. I realize if he does not get off his chair and come rescue me, my life is over. My simple respect for the lifeguard has shifted to desperate need.

We need the lifeguard at the beach; we need Jesus in every aspect of our lives. If I recognize the spiritual danger I'm in without Christ, I stop merely admiring him in a casual, abstract sense, and I begin to experience a deep, personal need for Christ as Saviour. This analogy will likely make it easy to transition into the third point of the *kerygma*, in which we talk about who Jesus is and what he came to do.

THIRD POINT: INTRODUCE JESUS

After all the talk of sin and separation, the next step—reconciliation—will be welcome.

Jesus is the one who restores our relationship with God. If we want to invite someone to open their heart to conversion, we need to be really clear on Christ—who he is and what he's done for us. There's lots of confusion surrounding the identity of Jesus in today's world, so this clarification is especially important.

"Jesus is God." This short statement is often the start of the confusion. Billions of people do not recognize the divinity of Jesus, and may not even understand that the Church proposes Christ's divinity. Unfortunately, this is true even for some Catholics. It's true for people within our families, among our friends and beyond.

When I discuss this misunderstanding with people in the Church, it often startles them. Recently, I spoke to a group of priests about evangelization, and I shocked them by suggesting that more than 85% of Catholics (even practicing Catholics) do not believe in—or are at least uncertain about—the divinity of Christ. I explained that I came to this conclusion by simply asking thousands of Catholics, "Do you believe that Jesus is God?" The answers I received ranged from, "No, I do not believe that he is God," to, "He is the son of God, but not God." There were those who said they believe he is God for us as Christians, but not necessarily for those of other religions. And a response I found particularly surprising, coming from a Catholic: "I have never heard such a claim."

Upset by this conclusion, one priest said, "I've been a parish priest for a long time, and I always assumed that my people, who cared enough to show up on Sunday, believed in the divinity of Christ." I empathize with him; it's a sad realization.

This realization strikes at the very heart of our faith—the great mystery of God coming to us, wanting to restore a relationship with his children. If we deny the divinity of Christ, most everything we believe in crumbles. The Sacraments, the Scriptures and the Church itself lose their meaning. The creed that the Church confesses is empty.

Remember the words of JPII: our faith communities and each of us as individuals "draw [their] origin and life from the personal response of each believer" *(Redemptoris Missio)* to what the Church preaches about Jesus Christ. So if a significant number of our people do not believe this confession of faith or are confused by it, is it any wonder that people leave the Church? Or that people attend Mass but are indifferent, disengaged from the community or at odds with the Church on many of her teachings? A building cannot stand without its cornerstone. Without Christ as the cornerstone, the faith loses its relevance and people become disengaged.

By now, there should be no question: properly understanding Christ's identity is critical. In our conversations, then, we can't make assumptions. Don't assume someone knows what the Church confesses to be true; make sure of it.

Belief in the divinity of Christ changes everything. Even if our faith feels tiny, we're open to Jesus. Jesus did not come to us merely to comfort us and teach us some important lessons, however wonderful that might sound. He came to save us—to bridge the gap between humanity and God, in order for us to have this personal relationship with God. In the words of JPII, "It is necessary to awaken again in believers a full relationship with Christ, mankind's only Saviour ..." (Address to the Bishops of Southern Germany, December 4, 1992).

As a related point, some Catholics might have heard that Jesus is God, but they still might not understand why this matters. In our kerygmatic proclamation, we have the opportunity to help them put the pieces of the puzzle together. Only a Christ who was fully human could experience mortality on the cross. Equally, only a Christ who was fully divine could possibly compensate by his death for all of humanity's sin. Only God could pay the price for us. And for God, death could never have the final word: the Resurrection seals our faith in Christ as Lord.

I've found that practicing, and even non-practicing, Catholics have at least some degree of reverence and respect for Christ. That's a good start; respect is important. But if they stop there, a lack of awareness of their need for Christ will seriously affect their spiritual life. If God is an aspect of their lives, but they don't think they actually need Him until a serious problem arises, it's time to answer the question, "Why Jesus?"

THE BRIDGE ANALOGY, PART THREE

To introduce this answer using the bridge analogy, begin by quoting John 3:16: "For God so loved the world that he gave his only Son, so that everyone who believes in him may not perish but may have eternal life."

Draw a line from God to man. Then ask, "What did Jesus take with him on the cross?" Once you have determined that it was *sin*, cross the word out.

Follow up with, "What did Jesus do on the third day?" (You can return to a Gospel passage if the person is not familiar with biblical accounts of Christ.) At this point you can cross out *death*.

Emphasize that Jesus takes away all our sins. We don't have to carry the burden of past decisions. Here, you may want to share your personal experience of God's mercy found in Jesus Christ. Let them know that there is great freedom in being forgiven and accepting mercy. Let them know about the joy of no longer feeling the separation between us and God. (You can cross out the word *separation*.) Let them know that knowing Christ changes the way you relate to him and his Church.

Finish drawing the crucifix on the paper by adding the horizontal beam (and a corpus, if you can). Now stand back and let them see how St. Catherine's bridge image shows how the cross becomes the bridge that gets us across the river. Check in to see how they're feeling—it's important for them to feel the good news that has followed the bad.

Imagine hearing, for the first time, somebody articulately explain the relevance of Jesus. He took our sins, which led to our freedom. He destroyed death so we can have hope. He reconciled us back to the Father so we can have access to God. This message should bring tremendous relief and appreciation.

With the right information, the person might now be ready, able and willing to commit their "... whole self freely to God, offering the full submission of intellect and will to God who reveals ... and freely assenting to the truth revealed by Him ..." *(Dei Verbum)*.

And you're ready to walk alongside them as they make that commitment.

FOURTH POINT: INVITATION TO RESPOND

We are now going to focus in on the end goal of evangelization. That is, we'll look at how to invite people to respond and experience firsthand the joy of being a son or daughter of the Father. As we prepare for our part in this sacred moment, let's reflect by making it personal.

It's nice to receive an invitation to a friend's wedding, anniversary or any other special function, isn't it? Sometimes this is most striking when that doesn't happen. I remember sitting around a table, talking with friends about the extravagant wedding plans of a mutual friend. It was going to be the event of the season! Inside, I lamented that I would not be able to enjoy the event, since I hadn't been invited. Sure, I appreciated the work that was being put into it, but I was on the outside looking in.

That changed the next day when the couple invited me. Suddenly, I had a whole new appreciation and excitement for the day because I was going to share it with them.

Similarly, it is inspiring to hear how good God is, but it is a whole other thing to be invited to experience it firsthand.

CALLED DEEPER INTO RELATIONSHIP: CATHOLICS WANT MORE

A number of years ago, when my family was living in Saskatoon, the evangelical preacher Billy Graham came to town. There was a big push for Catholics to get involved, and many people attended. After the event, I was asked to speak to the priests in the diocese about it.

Many of those I spoke to criticized the event, especially the altar call— the moment when the preacher invited people to come to the front and invite Christ into their lives. One priest recognized some of his own parishioners as they approached the altar, and he commented to this group of fellow priests that they were active parishioners. They were not the "unsaved," as Billy Graham's outreach suggested. It was not people who were lost who went forward to the altar; it was the faithful. From this priest's perspective, the event had been a waste of time.

I responded with a question: "Why did those faithful Catholics feel a need to go to the event and to go forward to give their lives to Christ?" He had no real answer, other than a suggestion that they were just following the crowd. Unwilling to accept his disregard for their authenticity, I put forward the possibility that they may be wanting more out of their relationship with Christ.

Consider this: Why are so many Catholics leaving the Church for non-Catholic Christian churches? We can tend to assume it's something superficial, like a different kind of music or a more engaging style of preaching. But I suspect that often, the real answer is these other churches let them experience some significant aspect of authentic Christian life that they did not recognize was available in their Catholic parishes. If this is so, our response should be to reflect critically on our expression of faith, understanding that authentic Catholic faith *does* provide people with what their hearts are made for: a personal, intimate relationship with God.

Again we go back to the words of Benedict XVI: "Christianity is not 'a new philosophy or a new form of morality,' but an encounter with the person of Christ, an event that ignites a personal relationship with Him" (General Audience, September 3, 2008). We must offer people an opportunity to open their lives to Christ, and we must celebrate and support that decision by bringing them into the community and a solid sacramental life. If we do this, our people will not wander in search of conversion, support and community outside of the Church.

Let's review what we have done so far in sharing our faith with a friend. We have "proclaimed with great spiritual power" the *kerygma*. We have laid out the truth: our relationship with God was broken by our sin, but Jesus—who is God—restored this relationship by his life, death and resurrection. Hopefully, through the Holy Spirit, we have brought the person to a point where they can open their heart to a Christ-centered life. Here, things get exciting ... and intimidating.

BE BOLD IN THE FACE OF SPIRITUAL BATTLE

It's at the point of *invitation* that things may get uncomfortable. The spiritual battle will intensify. From experience, I warn you that you might start looking for a way out. I remember working with a student—let's call him Jim—a number of years back. Jim had a great desire to be closer to God, but he felt that there was a wall between himself and God. Week after week, I would reiterate to Jim that God wanted to be in a personal relationship with him. Point by point, I would explain who Jesus was and what he had done for us on the cross. And every time, we would arrive at a "turning point." But rather than pray with Jim right there, I would send him home to the quiet of his room where he could open his heart to Jesus. And, over and over again, nothing changed for Jim.

One day, Jim dropped by the Catholic chapel in the campus to pray, and was surprised to find the Church filled with evangelical Protestant students. He stayed, listening attentively to the pastor who was recalling the life and faith of a student who had died a year earlier. Jim was struck by how the pastor described this student's personal and dynamic relationship with Christ. Jim left that chapel wanting what that other student had.

Instead of calling me for help, he sought out an evangelical friend. Jim's friend knew what he was looking for and how to deal with the "wall" Jim saw. He quickly invited Jim over to talk and, unlike when Jim met with me, he was not sent home to pray. Instead, his friend led him in a prayer of conversion. That night, Jim opened his heart to Christ.

The next day, I saw Jim on campus. As he walked towards me, I could see that something had changed in him. He could not wait to tell me how the wall had come down. He was eager to share the joy he felt in his new relationship with Christ.

I was thrilled for him! But I also recognized what had been lacking in my own outreach. His evangelical friend believed that when you desire a relationship with Christ, you can simply call out to him and he will respond. My hesitation to pray with Jim exposed my lack of faith that God would hear and answer us. I vowed that day that I would never send anyone home like I did with Jim. I have since been privileged to witness hundreds of Catholics experience conversion as I invite them to open their lives to a relationship with Christ.

THE RELATIONSHIP DIAGRAMS

Another visual tool will help us make the invitation in a clear and non-threatening way. The "relationship diagrams" below are a powerful tool to help your friend see the decision before them and to outline a way to respond appropriately. Fundamentally, the intention is to invite them to move from Christ being *outside* or *part of* their lives to Christ being *at the centre* of their lives. Spiritually, we can say this is "the point of bringing about repentance of sin, conversion of hearts and a decision of faith" (The New Evangelization for the Transmission of the Christian Faith).

These images can be powerful. Reflect on the explanation below so that when the time comes, your explanation will be natural and led by the Holy Spirit.

Step 1: Remind your friend of the bridge illustration. Focus on how Jesus provides a bridge to get to God. As of this point, though, we remain on the other side, still separated from God. What Jesus has accomplished does not automatically change our lives—it isn't imposed on us. It's an invitation to put our faith and life in his hands as we cross over the bridge.

What do we mean by "putting our faith" in God? We mean trusting in Jesus and what he did. We mean securely believing that Jesus is God and that his death took away our sins, freed us from death and made it possible for us to know and be in relationship with the Trinity. Stepping over the bridge is saying "yes" to these things. The images introduce a way of taking that step, of saying "yes."

Step 2: It will be helpful for them see the images in light of the answers to the following question that Professor Peter Kreeft often asked his students, and which you may want to ask your friend: "If you were to die and stand before Jesus and he asked, 'Why should I let you into heaven?', what would be your response?"

Peter Kreeft found that most Catholics present a resumé of what they have or have not done. They rarely mention Jesus. He concluded that Catholics may get to heaven, but they won't know how they got there. The sad realization he had was that most Catholics feel salvation is based on a resumé rather than what Jesus has done.

Step 3: Begin by describing the *top three images*, which represent levels of commitment in three kinds of human relationships. Explain how the first image represents *someone who is single*; there is no romantic relationship in their life. The second image represents *someone who is dating*; the relationship is part of their life, but commitment is limited. The third image represents *someone who is married*; there is an intimate relationship and a permanent mutual commitment.

Move to the *bottom three images*, which represent levels of commitment in a relationship with God. The first image represents *someone who does not have a relationship with Jesus*. As far as this person is concerned, Jesus is outside their life. The second image describes *someone who has Jesus as part of their life*. Emphasize that this is not an indictment on the character of the person, nor a judgement on how much they do or don't sin—it marks the relevance and role of their relationship with Christ. The third is *someone with a Christ-centered life* who desires to direct all aspects of their life to Christ.

With this third image, stress that we are not talking about perfection, neither in the top three images nor the bottom three. We're talking about a relationship in which the person aims to live more and more for the other. At the start of this kind of relationship, there may be a lot of stumbling. But, over time, if the person is truly committed to the relationship, it can grow to a beautiful experience of communion.

Step 4: At this point, focus on the bottom three images and ask them what they see as the difference between a person in image two and a person in image three. They will have many great insights. You want them to understand that *trust* is the main difference, which has a direct impact on the levels of commitment we have in our relationship with God.

To clarify, I would refer back to the responses to Peter Kreeft's question. You can now ask the question, "If the person in the second image died and stood before Jesus, what would he say?" The common and obvious answer is that they would present their spiritual resumé: "I've never done anything that bad. A lot of things I've done were very good." On the other hand, the person in the third image would say, "It's not what I've done; it's what Jesus has done for me." You could say the difference between the two is trust. One trusts in their resumé to get them to heaven, while the other trusts in Christ.

Step 5: In light of all the discussions you have had about *kerygma*, now is the time to ask three questions. The first is to ask the person which image, out of the bottom three, best represents their current life. Often, they answer with the first or second image. The second question is where they would *like* to be. The common response—thank God!—is the third image. The third question, then, which invites conversion, is if they would like to move from whichever image they currently see themselves in to the third image. *Ask if they'd like to put Christ at the centre of their life.*

These questions are very important because they invite the person to engage with the images and with you. By asking these questions, we're not telling them where they are, or where they should be, or how to get to where they want to be. Instead, we're inviting them into the most important element of conversion, according to St. Augustine's *Confessions:* self-reflection. Only in honest self-reflection can anybody come to see their own doubts, struggles, fears, weakness, pride, etc. Being mindful of how far we have fallen enables us to discover God's relentless and abundant mercies.

The first question, "Which image best represents your life?", asks them to assess, based on the images, their current spiritual state. They reflect on their present reality as they see it, based on the content or the truth of the *kerygma* that has been presented to them. This place of honest self-reflection is a place that most have not visited. It is necessary for them to know where they are in order to move forward in their relationship with Jesus.

Knowledge of their present spiritual reality opens the way for them to knowing how to answer the second question, "Where would you like to be in relationship with Jesus?" From there they can determine, based on their understanding of the *kerygma,* where their heart's desire lies. This reflection is not on the do's and don'ts, on the past and present, or on failures and weaknesses. This isn't the time for them to compare themselves with the most mature religious person they may know, or to consider the seemingly impossible task of becoming like Mother Teresa. It is an invitation to answer the question, "What is it that you desire?" In this place of honest self-assessment, a person is ready to make a well-thought-out and intentional decision about whether they want to place Christ at the centre of their life.

DECISION

We are at a very critical moment here. It would be wise to stop and reflect on what we are inviting our friend to do: to move from God being just a part of their life to God being at the center. Such a decision will change how they relate and engage in their relationship with Jesus and his Church. It will impact their eternal destiny, not to mention their earthly life and the people around them. The angels and saints will be hanging on every word, interceding and anticipating the possible return of a prodigal soul. Their return will be cause for great rejoicing.

We'll invite them to move to a Christ-centred relationship by saying "yes," opening their heart in prayer directed to God. They will use words that clearly express their intention and desire to place Christ at the centre of their life.

Recall all our previous discussion of the analogy of marriage in relationship to conversion. This is the moment when we are waiting, with God, for this person's response to a profound invitation of love. We are waiting, prayerfully, for their "yes."

REPENTANCE

Fundamentally, to invite someone to cross over the bridge is to "proclaim with great spiritual power to the point of bringing about repentance of sin, conversion of hearts and a decision of faith" (The New

Evangelization for the Transmission of the Christian Faith). Repentance comes up often in our human relationships. I know if I do something wrong, I need to say sorry. I need to repent. Here, we're talking about repentance as the fundamental recognition of our need for God. More specifically, it is a recognition of our need for Jesus.

St. Ambrose speaks of two conversions in the Church: "water and tears: the water of Baptism and the tears of repentance" (CCC 1429). The conversion of tears requires us to articulate an intentional response of repentance. Is God limited by a certain response? No, of course not. But in our highly secularized society, an unambiguous response to God stands out. It is not the nature of love and relationship to simply sit still, unresponsive, while someone offers love to us. Love always calls out for love.

Below is a prayer you can invite your friend to make their own. It encompasses "repentance of sin, conversion of hearts and a decision of faith":

> Father, I believe that you know me and love me. I have not always chosen to love you, and have broken my relationship with you through my sins. Thank you for sending your Son Jesus who proved your love for me on the cross.

> Lord Jesus, I open the door of my heart and invite you to be the centre of my life—to be my Saviour and my Lord. Direct me by your Holy Spirit and help me to live the Gospel with my whole life. Amen.

OR

> Jesus, I know that you are the Son of God and have given your life for me. I want to follow you faithfully and to be led by your word. You know me and you love me. I place my trust in you and I put my whole life into your hands. I want you to be the power that strengthens me and the joy which never leaves me.

I've heard people ask, "Are these prayers Catholic?" Well, the Church asks us to make a decision of faith, and these prayers let us express that decision. For a clear Catholic precedent, consider Pope Benedict XVI's homily at World Youth Day Madrid in 2011. He spoke of having a personal relationship with Christ. Such a relationship, he said, is not a result of human effort, that prideful spiritual resumé. He was clear that it is a personal decision that is needed. He said,

... faith is not the result of human effort, of human reasoning, but rather a gift of God: "Blessed are you, Simon son of Jonah! For flesh and blood has not revealed this to you, but my Father in heaven." Faith starts with God, who opens his heart to us and invites us to share in his own divine life. Faith does not simply provide information about who Christ is; rather, it entails a personal relationship with Christ, a surrender of our whole person, with all our understanding, will and feelings, to God's self-revelation. So Jesus' question: "But who do you say that I am?", is ultimately a challenge to the disciples to make a personal decision in his regard.

Pope Benedict then went on to call for a response. He did not presume the people knew how to respond. He invited everyone to "say to [Jesus]" who they believed he was, to pray using clear words of intent. The young people were being invited to say something to Jesus:

> Dear young people, today Christ is asking you the same question which he asked the Apostles: "Who do you say that I am?" Respond to him with generosity and courage, as befits young hearts like your own. Say to him: "Jesus, I know that you are the Son of God, who have given your life for me. I want to follow you faithfully and to be led by your word. You know me and you love me. I place my trust in you and I put my whole life into your hands. I want you to be the power that strengthens me and the joy which never leaves me." (Homily at World Youth Day Madrid)

The homily ended there. It seems Pope Benedict believed the prayer could accomplish a response. When we are in conversations with people, we need to respect what we are inviting them to do, and believe that God will meet them there.

Another objection people might have is that it sounds too simple. A person just says this prayer and there it is, conversion? Of course there is a lifetime of ongoing conversion and spiritual maturation ahead of each person. But as Catholics, we see how seemingly ordinary things are made extraordinary all the time. Think of a baptism: in this sacrament, we witness something that seems simple achieve an eternal impact.

For others, it may seem prideful or presumptuous to say, "Christ is at the centre of my life." To help overcome this hesitation, let us go back to Peter Kreeft's question: "If you were to die and stand before the gates of heaven and Jesus asked, 'Why should I let you in?', how would you respond?" If you had the perspective that it was about your resumé, then yes, it would be prideful to suggest that you have mastered the Christian life. But if you understand that Jesus is the one who made it possible for you to approach him, then it is true humility that allows you to have Jesus in your life's centre. As St. Paul says, "May I never boast of anything except the cross of our Lord Jesus Christ" (Galatians 6:14).

To dispel any doubts of how God responds to our cry, recall St. Augustine's conversion in the *Confessions*, which we examined in a previous section. His friend Ponticianus, a person just like you, led him to choose to trust completely in God's mercy. Ponticianus shared the stories of two men who converted immediately after reading the life of St. Anthony. Ponticianus pointed out that St. Anthony's story instantly touched their hearts, and they chose to turn away from those things of the world that had a hold on them. In a moment, they turned their lives over to the service of God.

God used this testimony to turn Augustine's thoughts inward. In those two men, Augustine saw what he was unwilling to do—give himself fully to God. Augustine cried out to the friend who was listening to this story with him, "What is the matter with us?" He saw those converts taking "heaven by force" while he continued to resist giving in to God.

St. Augustine fled to the house's garden, weeping. But then, prompted by the Holy Spirit, he returned to his friend, opened the Scriptures and began to read the first page his eyes landed on:

> "... let us live honorably as in the day, not in revelling and drunkenness, not in debauchery and licentiousness, not in quarreling and jealousy. Instead, put on the Lord Jesus Christ, and make no provision for the flesh, to gratify its desires" (Romans 13:13-14). Then, "[i]nstantly at the end of the sentence, by a light as it were, of serenity infused into my heart—all the gloom of doubt vanished away."

These dramatic, profound moments aren't constrained to gardens. They can and will happen in ordinary places. I've been privileged to witness them.

Take this example from a popular coffee and sandwich shop. As I was sharing the *kerygma* with a young man I'll call Jake, we were interrupted twice by friends coming to greet us. Each time we easily returned to our discussion. It was natural because his heart was being moved by the truth of the *kerygma*. In the midst of noise and activity all around us, I leaned in and asked him if he wanted to place Christ at the centre of his life. With great sincerity, he said, "Yes, I want him in my life." So we prayed right there and then, loud enough for Jake and me to hear, but indiscernible to anyone else.

I bumped into Jake more than a decade later. He's now married with kids. He shared with me how that moment in the coffee shop was the beginning of his faith life, the one that is now being shared with his wife and his family.

With clear understanding, therefore, confidently ask your friend if they would like to place Christ at the centre of their life. Give them time to reflect. If they respond positively, you can ask them to follow along with you as you pray or have them use their own words in prayer. Or you may want to have a resource like CCO's *Ultimate Relationship* booklet or a similar prayer on hand so they can read it themselves as a prayer to God. The important thing is that the prayer clearly states their intention of opening their heart to Christ. If you are praying and getting them to follow, I suggest you keep it brief. You may feel comfortable and desire to go on in prayer, but that may not be the case for them. Remember, in this moment, it's all about them.

CHAPTER 4:
AFTER THE INVITATION—
GOING FROM HERE

The late Father Bob Bedard, founder of the Companions of the Cross, saw the process of evangelization as "something we start and God finishes. The proclamation is human, the response is human. But what follows is divine" (Only God Can Change a Human Heart).

After you invite someone to respond prayerfully to Christ's invitation, and as this person makes this prayer, you should know that God is hearing that most humble of prayers, "Come to me ... I need you." When they are done praying, ask them what they think, how they feel. However they're feeling, it is the evangelist's job to help solidify what God has done.

Sometimes a conversion is accompanied by intense emotions. Other times, there aren't any strong feelings associated with the experience. Both experiences are totally valid, and acknowledging this can help people stay true to the choice they've made. It's not how they felt at the time or how they feel afterwards that matters. Rather, it's the choice they made that brought them into the relationship.

To revisit the analogy I proposed in an early section of this book, we learn from the Catechism that it is not the good feelings and attractions that spouses feel toward one another that keep them together in good times and bad. It's the concrete, recorded and witnessed "yes" on the day of marriage, as well as the grace that comes from the sacrament, that hold the couple together in good times and in hard times. Similarly, it is not our pleasant spiritual feelings that indicate the reality of our closeness with God, but our choice to let Him be the centre of our lives, and His faithful response to that choice.

After witnessing your friend's momentous "yes," emphasize that God honours their decision. He acted whether or not they feel anything. They need to know that even when they fail—and we all fail—God is merciful and committed to the relationship. Similar to a marriage relationship, failure does not spell the end of the relationship, but an opportunity to say sorry and to receive forgiveness. Properly understood, love gives you the freedom to fail, the freedom to be yourself. Through God's grace, they will be able to mature and overcome those areas of weakness or sin. Help them to see these truths and show that there is good reason to be hopeful and confident.

Your witness, love and accompaniment will also go a long way in protecting this person from spiritual attack following initial conversion. We know that a conversion of heart and change of life is real. We also recognize the reality that the evil one comes to "steal and kill and destroy" (John 10:10). In Matthew 13, Jesus, in a parable, speaks of how the seed of faith can be choked up very quickly if not planted in good soil:

> The one on whom seed was sown on the rocky places, this is the man who hears the word and immediately receives it with joy; yet he has no firm root in himself, but is only temporary, and when affliction or persecution arises because of the word, immediately he falls away.

> And the one on whom seed was sown among the thorns, this is the man who hears the word, and the worry of the world and the deceitfulness of wealth choke the word, and it becomes unfruitful.

> And the one on whom seed was sown on the good soil, this is the man who hears the word and understands it; who indeed bears fruit and brings forth, some a hundredfold, some sixty, and some thirty. (Matthew 13:3-9; 20-23)

This parable has played out over and over again, and continues today. There is no easier and sweeter prey for the enemy than the soul that has just received the new seed of faith and relationship with Christ. When we're a witness to conversion, our responsibility is to ensure the word of God is planted in good soil in order to produce abundant fruit.

Two obvious and necessary components of this *good soil* are Christian community (the parish, Christian fellowship) and the Sacraments. We should immediately invite the person to participate in these, if they aren't doing so already. It is also paramount to provide a newly converted person with basic information on how to pray, read the Scriptures and live a Christian life. Furthermore, the book of the Acts of the Apostles, in the story of Pentecost, reminds us that while it is necessary to know Jesus, we also need to be filled with the Holy Spirit. Take the time to pray with them as soon as possible, and specifically ask for the Holy Spirit to come in power.

There's so much more you can do in that moment of conversion to help firmly root the new seed of faith in good soil. The fact that you are there sitting with them and witnessing their consent to place Christ at the centre of their life will go a long way in confirming the reality of their conversion. Make the decision to pray for your friend and to continue to intentionally accompany them following their first "yes" to Christ.

WHAT IF THEY SAY "NO"?

As we've reiterated many times, there is no possibility for an authentic "yes" if the person is not also free to say "no." There is the real possibility that the person we've been speaking with will say they're not ready to place Christ at the centre of their lives.

I want to pause here to emphasize that evangelists should never go in expecting a "no," no matter how unlikely a "yes" appears to our mortal eyes. Recall that God can do anything. Pray to the Holy Spirit; glorify God in his goodness by expecting great things from him. Wrestle inwardly for this person's soul along with the Lord. It's very likely your friend will be able to sense whether you think they'll be able to say "yes," and this may be what does or does not allow them the freedom to respond.

All the same, they are truly free to say "no," and we must respect this. If they do, this is where prophetic listening becomes very important. Listen to the reasons they give for saying "no." There may be room for more spiritual conversation right then and there, followed by a reiteration of the invitation—for example, if it becomes clear that the person thinks they have to be perfect before they can respond to God's love.

On the other hand, you may realize, for example, that this person is still a long way from trusting God, despite intellectually grasping the message of the Gospel as you've presented it, and does not feel free to give a "yes" quite yet.

Make prayerful, prophetic listening your priority, and don't be too quick to abandon the conversation. Remember that everyone *does* in fact desire Christ, in their heart of hearts, and that many apparent objections may be "smokescreens" put up to avoid having to make a choice. But above all, always demonstrate genuine love, and always make it clear by your words and actions that your concern for them and interest in them are by no means conditional on their willingness to say "yes" to Christ.

Regardless of how they answer, our job as evangelists is to continue to accompany them, lovingly and intentionally, in their journey towards the Lord. We should never be afraid or embarrassed to obey the promptings of the Holy Spirit in reiterating this invitation throughout our relationship with anyone, even if they say "no" many times. In faith, we need to hope and plan with the Lord in his love for each soul.

CELEBRATE CONVERSION

The good news for evangelists is that God *does* act, and conversions *do* happen. And conversions should be celebrated! Ultimately, that celebration doesn't always happen. Downplaying or overlooking a person's conversion is a common experience. It speaks to an underlying attitude of misunderstanding or failing to appreciate conversion.

Recall how, in my breakdown of reasons why Catholics may not be manifesting the fruit of initial conversion (earlier in this book), I suggested that sometimes the problem is they aren't confident in the reality of their conversion because no one affirmed them in it. I recently had an intense experience of this when I was invited to speak at a retreat. The hall was filled with people, and my job was to invite people to put Christ at the centre of their lives. At the end of the presentation, I did just that—invited them to open their hearts and place Christ at the centre.

Later that evening, a woman came and asked if I would talk to her sister. For the next fifteen minutes, I sat with this woman's sister, fielding objection after objection from her with regard to saying "yes" to the faith. All these objections seemed more like smokescreens to me, so instead of continuing to focus on them, trusting in the Holy Spirit, I decided to go straight to the question, "Would you want to have Christ at the centre of your life?" She stopped objecting, reflected for a moment, and then she said, "Yes, I would." So right there, in the midst of all the people running around in the church hall, we prayed together.

After the prayer, there was a newness in her face. She tearfully described how her heart was full of joy. She felt as if Christ had entered into her heart. It was a beautiful moment.

Recognizing the significance of this moment, I called the parish priest over to hear what she'd experienced. After listening to this woman who had been lost and dead spiritually and now was alive, his only response was, "I hope I will see you at Mass tomorrow." There was no acknowledgment of conversion, no celebration of the return of this soul. I was devastated.

I'm relieved to report that this young lady continues to grow in her faith and in her involvement in her parish. But I'm sad to say it wasn't because her conversion was acknowledged, remembered and celebrated by the priest and the community. It's actually *despite* a lack of those things. Involvement—her pastor's first concern—is a good thing, but we can't forget the conversion that makes it possible.

Consider this: While parish involvement is one obvious fruit of conversion, we must also remember that this is not the *reason* we desire people's conversion. Our desire is the Father's desire: that each of these souls come back to him and remain with him throughout all eternity. It's something much more profound than participation in parish ministries, necessary as that is to the life of the Church. If we believe this, how can we *not* celebrate?

CCO's campus ministry communities are a beautiful example of what is possible when conversion is celebrated. The campuses have a strong sense of community, and a culture of conversion is growing. To me, this is because their leaders showcase conversion. They value it, they are able to identify it and they work hard to invite others to conversion.

CONVERSION CONSEQUENCES

> After [the encounter with Jesus Christ], everything is different as a result of *metanoia*, that is, the state of conversion strongly urged by Jesus himself (cf. Mk 1:15). In a personal encounter with Jesus Christ, faith takes the form of a relationship with him. (The New Evangelization for the Transmission of the Christian Faith)

There are three parables in Luke 15: the lost coin, the lost sheep and the prodigal son. In each of them, there is great rejoicing when "the Lost" has been found. When you're talking with someone and they decide to place Christ at the center of their life, there is cause for rejoicing. We learn from the Father in the parable of the prodigal son why there so much rejoicing: "For this son of mine was dead and is alive again; he was lost and is found" (Luke 15:24).

When we talk about returning to our Heavenly Father, it's more than a religious sentiment; it is a spiritual reality. This encounter brings us into a personal relationship with Jesus Christ. It marks a conversion of heart. We learn from the Church that nothing will be the same after this encounter—and that claim is supported by countless testimonies, including mine. I fell in love with God in a moment's time, and my heart was captured and transformed.

When we consider what grace has accomplished in a new convert's life, we should expect that "[a]fter this encounter, everything [will be] different as a result of *metanoia*, that is, the state of conversion" (The New Evangelization for the Transmission of the Christian Faith). What change in their spiritual life should we expect?

LOVE OF SCRIPTURE, LOVE OF PRAYER, AND SANCTITY IN DAILY LIFE

My own conversion story, shared earlier in this book, illustrates how the Holy Spirit continues his work following our conversion. Walking out of the Church after I'd had a profound encounter with God, I was filled with inexplicable joy. I did not want it to end—I began to sing in my car. The next day, moved by the Holy Spirit, I went to a bookstore and bought a tiny Bible that contained the Psalms and the New Testament. I read it every night. I was so inspired I couldn't put it down.

When I was eight years old, early on my journey towards conversion, I made a decision to pray each night. For the most part, I kept that promise. Yet after my conversion, prayer took on a whole new life. Many students reflect this experience back to me: "It's as if I am really talking to God and he is listening," one said. After conversion, people welcome an invitation to pray every day—even a challenge to pray an hour each day isn't too much to ask.

Prior to my conversion, there would be little in my life that would give testimony to a life of sanctity. I was, without reservation, living in the world. Yet after my conversion, even without a priest or mentor to guide me, I was given the grace to spontaneously want to change my ways. That grace changed my life. Now, I certainly haven't mastered my life of sanctity, but I can confidently say that compared to the way I was before my conversion, I am a new man, living a new life.

I don't state these things to suggest that I'm an unusually pious or holy Catholic. In my experience, this response is typical of someone experiencing the fruits of conversion. God pours out these graces on his children. As evangelists, we should recognize these gifts, celebrate them, and cultivate them when they begin to appear in others.

LOVE OF THE CHURCH

Along with an encounter of the heart, the Holy Spirit "open[s] the eyes of the mind" *(Dei Verbum)* so that as someone encounters Christ, they also develop a new and deep appreciation for the truth of Christ and his Church. This appreciation often comes naturally with surprising ease and profound clarity.

It's through this grace of the Holy Spirit "opening the eyes of the mind and giving 'joy and ease to everyone in assenting to the truth and believing in it'" *(Dei Verbum)* that we come to believe. This is an important truth that we must not pass over lightly. It's well-known that people in today's society struggle with the Church, its teachings and its views, especially on controversial matters. Yes, it's important to be compelling witnesses to truth and to offer sound arguments for Church teachings when we can. But beyond these faithful attempts, we recognize that truth can only be understood with the help of the Holy Spirit. As St. Paul reminds us,

> No, we declare God's wisdom, a mystery that has been hidden and that God destined for our glory before time began ... What we have received is not the spirit of the world, but the Spirit who is from God, so that we may understand what God has freely given us. This is what we speak, not in words taught us by human wisdom but in words taught by the Spirit, explaining spiritual realities with Spirit-taught words. The person without the Spirit does not accept the things that come from the Spirit of God but considers them foolishness, and cannot understand them because they are discerned only through the Spirit. (1 Corinthians 2: 7-15)

Teachings that may have seemed impossible to believe, irrelevant or easy to dismiss by someone prior to their conversion take on a new beauty, relevance and necessity following conversion. While there may be a good deal of catechesis that the person still needs before they can feel confident in their understanding of Church teachings, we can expect them to exhibit a fresh openness, trust and desire to understand and live out these teachings.

JOYFUL WITNESS

We can't give what we don't have. When we consider the mission of the Church to bring Christ to the world, we'll be silent unless we have personal knowledge and experience of a living God. The story of the Samaritan woman at the well in John's Gospel speaks to the evangelical zeal that flows instantly from an encounter with Jesus Christ:

> When a Samaritan woman came to draw water, Jesus said to her, "Will you give me a drink?" (His disciples had gone into the town to buy food.) ... Jesus [said], "If you knew the gift of God and who it is that asks you for a drink, you would have asked him and he would have given you living water ... Everyone who

drinks this water will be thirsty again, but whoever drinks the water I give them will never thirst. Indeed, the water I give them will become in them a spring of water welling up to eternal life." The woman said to him, "Sir, give me this water so that I won't get thirsty and have to keep coming here to draw water."

The woman said, "I know that Messiah" (called Christ) "is coming. When he comes, he will explain everything to us." Then Jesus declared, "I, the one speaking to you—I am he ..."

Then, leaving her water jar, the woman went back to the town and said to the people, "Come, see a man who told me everything I ever did. Could this be the Messiah?" They came out of the town and made their way toward him ... (John 4:7-15; 25-26; 28-30; 39-41)

We see how the Samaritan woman's encounter with Jesus had a significant impact on the life of the community. Good news: your friend's conversion will have a similar influence in their parish and community. Joy is contagious!

A compelling testimony draws people to meet Jesus for themselves ... and then go back to bring others. Consider the reach of St. Augustine's powerful conversion story. Who knows how many souls have turned to Christ because of this testimony? A person's witness to how God has impacted their life can revive a listener's failing faith. The message people hear is that God is alive and active, and they are given hope that they, too, might encounter God. A testimony can map out a pathway for conversion.

THE CATHOLIC EXPERIENCE OF CONVERSION

Soon after my conversion in 1982, I began to search for Catholics who shared my experience. Unfortunately, in those early days, I found none.

The agent for transmitting the faith is the universal Church ... In past decades, the local Churches have done their utmost in this field ... Yet, "the cultural climate and the general state of fatigue in many Christian communities in our local Churches is endangering the proclamation of the faith, its transmission to others and instruction in the faith ... Indeed, a "new evangelization" is often synonymous with dynamic functioning, with "renewed spiritual efforts in the life of faith within the local Churches ..." (The New Evangelization for the Transmission of the Christian Faith)

At first, being alone allowed me to develop strong friendships with two evangelical Christians. Giving in to their relentless invitations, one night I went to a "College and Career" event hosted by their church. I was overwhelmed by the sheer number of students who went out of their way to welcome me. In conversations with them, I was struck by their love and devotion to Jesus. They were unashamed and filled with an inspired boldness and urgency to make Jesus known. I was impressed, and this experience eventually inspired me, along with my wife Angele, to start a movement based on the most lasting takeaways from that experience—a love for Jesus and a love for mission.

Although I was inspired to unimaginable heights during this period, I was also brought to the depths of heartbreak. Each of my conversations would inevitably lead to the fact that I was Catholic. It seemed that every second non-Catholic Christian I met would respond by letting me know that they had once been Catholic. Past tense. They would explain in detail how their life was impacted when they encountered Jesus Christ as their personal Lord and Saviour. What they were suggesting, essentially, was that they felt they'd had to leave the Catholic Church to encounter Christ.

In that moment, I wanted to drop to my knees and beg them to come back. "We need your love for Jesus and missionary zeal!" I wanted to shout. I searched and searched for a place—a Catholic environment— to which I could bring them, one that would live up to their present experience of the Christian faith. And at that time, I was not about to suggest the parish I went to each Sunday. From what I saw, there was very little going on at my parish that would resemble anything close to the expression of love and zeal for Christ and mission I saw at that first Friday night event. I remember saying to God as a third-year student, "I want to do something about this. Use me."

Today, many years later, I'm happy to say I'd have a ready answer to my search. I know that within the Catholic Church, in parishes all throughout the world, each person *can* live out a personal relationship with Christ, as a Catholic. I now know, too, that thousands of Catholics share my heart for souls and my prayer that God would use them. I see the emphases the bishops are placing on evangelization and conversion:

> The "first proclamation" is where the kerygma, the message of salvation of the paschal mystery of Jesus Christ, is proclaimed with great spiritual power to the point of bringing about repentance of sin, conversion of hearts and a decision of faith. (The New Evangelization for the Transmission of the Christian Faith)

Yet there is still much work to be done. I recommend that these words coming from the bishops become the mission statement of every diocese, parish and individual Catholic person. They say it all. Focus in on one small section: "to the point of bringing about ..." It is essential to understand the goal of evangelization: creating a concrete opportunity for people to respond, to give their consent.

As I've reiterated throughout the pages of this book, a "yes" brings about a profound, life-changing conversion. Such an evangelical shift within the Church will have a transformative impact on the life of our communities, "[f]or missionary activity renews the church, revitalizes the faith and Christian identity, and offers fresh enthusiasm and new incentive ... For in the Church's history, missionary drive has always been a sign of vitality" (*Redemptoris Missio*).

My hope is that these reflections leave Catholics with a deeper understanding of conversion, evangelization and being missionary, and a confidence in their ability to put this understanding into practice in their ministries and day-to-day lives. The Church calls the laity to embrace and fulfill Jesus' commission to go and make disciples of all nations. I'm inviting you to take these principles and tools to embrace the challenge to actively live out your missionary role within the Church—not being missionary merely by idea or conviction, but being missionary by action.

In the words of St. John Paul II:

God is opening before the Church the horizons of a humanity more fully prepared for the sowing of the Gospel. I sense that the moment has come to commit all of the Church's energies to a new evangelization and to the mission *ad gentes*. No believer in Christ, no institution of the Church can avoid this supreme duty: to proclaim Christ to all peoples. *(Redemptoris Missio)*

APPENDIX: TWO CCO RESOURCES— *THE ULTIMATE RELATIONSHIP* AND *DISCOVERY*

Throughout this book, I've emphasized the idea that intentional accompaniment and clear proclamation of the Gospel are keys to the New Evangelization. These are truths that go beyond any particular evangelical program or set of materials; they ought to be integrated into our overall attitudes as missionary disciples. Indeed, if we can't have intentional spiritual conversations with the people God puts in our lives, I'm skeptical that even our best-designed parish programs will bear fruit the way God intends.

That being said, good Catholic evangelical materials and programs can be a big help in terms of communicating the *kerygma* clearly and simply. CCO has been blessed to have had thousands of evangelical conversations over the years of our existence, and we've equipped our students to have these conversations both on campuses and throughout their lives after graduation. We've developed resources to help support and equip students to effectively have these conversations in different situations. Our two key resources to aid in a spiritual conversation are *The Ultimate Relationship* booklet and the *Discovery* Faith Study. I've included this description of these materials for any readers who may be interested in using them.

CCO created *The Ultimate Relationship* booklet, or *U.R.* for short, many years ago, when we felt the need to be able to condense the most important message of the Catholic faith into a format that met these requirements:

1. Easy for ANYONE to share

2. Clear, concise and complete

3. Able to actually lead people to an opportunity to make a clear act of faith or decision, not just discuss or talk about something

The *U.R.* is a pocket-sized booklet that can be shared within ten minutes. It can also be expanded upon if necessary. More importantly, it contains the clear and simple message of the Gospel in four points:

1. God created us for a relationship with Him

2. That relationship is broken through original sin

3. Jesus died on the Cross to restore our broken relationship

4. We are each personally invited to receive the gift of the restored relationship given to us by Jesus Christ

The booklet walks readers through a simple presentation of the Gospel, and culminates in a personally relevant series of images we call the "Relationship Diagrams," which enable people to identify their own position or convictions regarding Jesus Christ. The climax of the booklet is in an invitation for readers to make a concrete, personal commitment to Jesus through a prayer known as the "Commitment Prayer."

Here are some ideas to get you started with *The Ultimate Relationship*. If you are a parish priest or leader in a Catholic organization, these are some of the most common ways *The Ultimate Relationship* might be used in your context:

• Giving it to the leaders in your parish/organization so that they can use it in their ministry

• Training your leaders to effectively use *The Ultimate Relationship*, along with supplementary analogies and strategies, with help from someone who is an expert in *The Ultimate Relationship* (www.cco.ca)

• Giving it as a gift at Easter or Christmas to all of your parishioners, and instructing them how to use it

• Providing the content for a great homily, or homily series, on the core message of the Gospel

• Using *The Ultimate Relationship* in sacramental preparation, particularly for Baptism or Reconciliation

If you are interested in using *The Ultimate Relationship* in your personal life as a missionary disciple, and not necessarily in an official sense in your parish, here are three things you could do:

• Train yourself in using *The Ultimate Relationship* to share the Gospel clearly and simply

• Intentionally look for opportunities to share *The Ultimate Relationship* with those around you

• Give *The Ultimate Relationship* to someone else so that they can share the Gospel with others and show them how to use this resource

If you're looking for something a bit more substantial, CCO's *Discovery* Faith Study is a powerful tool for proclaiming the Gospel in a clear and simple way, one that invites people to enter a personal relationship with Jesus. The faith study is designed to be hosted in the context of a small group of four to eight participants with a leader. This small group setting allows for authentic fellowship and faith sharing to occur: small groups provide an environment where people can grow more comfortable talking about their faith. The *Discovery* study and the other four CCO faith studies (*Source, Growth, Obedience* and *Commission*) offer an intentional pathway that can help in accompanying people through an initial conversion to Christ and growth as missionary disciples.

The *Discovery* study is easily adaptable to various settings. You might consider starting one in your parish, in your neighbourhood or in your workplace. You could host it in your home, or a coffee shop, or in the parish.

Regardless of the context you choose, one key to starting a small-group faith study is the personal invitation: Following reflection and prayer, personally invite specific individuals to join the study (if possible, either in person or by phone). This is a simple but significant way to both reflect God's personal love for each participant and to build relationships based on trust. And, since impersonal invitations are easy to ignore, it also makes it more likely that the person will say "yes."

Discovery will likely take you about six weeks to complete with weekly meetings. CCO's website (www.cco.ca) provides resources for leading this faith study and getting the most out of it. Above all, however, let the attitudes I've encouraged throughout this book guide your leadership: intentionally accompany each participant, caring for their souls as God does, and work hard to make your communication of the Gospel as clear and simple as possible. Remember: Christ's love impels us to do this for them and for the souls they might someday reach.

BIBLIOGRAPHY

Augustine. *Confessions*. Trans. Edward B. Pusey. Christian Classics Ethereal Library. 2005. Web.

Bedard, Bob. Only God Can Change a Human Heart. Companions of the Cross. n.d. Web.

Benedict XVI. Apostolic Journey to Madrid on the occasion of the 26th World Youth Day. Final Mass Homily. Cuatro Vientos Airbase, Madrid. August 21, 2011. Libreria Editrice Vaticana. Web.

— Encyclical Letter, *Deus Caritas Est*. December 25, 2005. Libreria Editrice Vaticana. Web.

— General Audience. Paul VI Audience Hall. September 3, 2008. Libreria Editrice Vaticana. Web.

— General Audience. Paul VI Audience Hall. February 17, 2010. Libreria Editrice Vaticana. Web.

— General Audience. St. Peter's Square. October 21, 2009. Libreria Editrice Vaticana. Web.

Catechism of the Catholic Church. Libreria Editrice Vaticana. 1993. Web.

Francis. Apostolic Exhortation, *Evangelii Gaudium.* Libreria Editrice Vaticana. November 24, 2013. Web.

Intentional Accompaniment. Internal document. Catholic Christian Outreach, 2017.

John Paul II. Address to Bishops of Southern Germany on their *Ad Limina* visit. December 4, 1992. *L'Osservatore Romano* (English ed.) December 23, 1992. Print.

— *Discourse to the XIX Assembly of C.E.L.A.M.* (Port au Prince, 9 March 1983). *L'Osservatore Romano* (English ed.) 18 April 1983. Print.

— Encyclical Letter, *Redemptoris Missio: On the permanent validity of the Church's missionary mandate.* Libreria Editrice Vaticana. December 7, 1990. Web.

— Cited in Personal Relationship to Jesus According to John Paul II. *The Crossroads Initiative.* Jan 5, 2018. Web.

Paul VI. Dogmatic Constitution on Divine Revelation, *Dei Verbum.* Libreria Editrice Vaticana. November 18, 1965. Web.

Ratzinger, Joseph. *Pilgrim Fellowship of Faith: The Church as Communion.* Ed. Stephan Otto Horn and Vinzenz Pfnür; trans. Henry Taylor. San Francisco: Ignatius Press, 2005. Print.

Synod of Bishops. *Instrumentum Laboris.* The New Evangelization for the Transmission of the Christian Faith. XIII Ordinary General Assembly. The General Secretariat of the Synod of Bishops and Libreria Editrice Vaticana. Vatican City. 2012. Web.

Wedell, Sherry. *Forming Intentional Disciples: The Path to Knowing and Following Jesus.* Huntington, Ind.: Our Sunday Visitor, Inc. 2012. Print.